The Crazy Story of Uber

Sex, Scandal, and Billions of Dollars – A Silicon Valley Startup

By
Ryan Ewing

Table of Contents

Introduction

Telling the story of Uber is both easy enough and hard as hell. It's easy-peasy because there's so much written about it or related to it out there on the Internet and—gasp!—my Kindle that I don't even have to move my butt off a chair to know exactly where Travis Kalanick and Garrett Camp were hanging out on that fateful winter day when they conceived their brainchild. After all, this is the Information Age, and that bit of trivia is just a click, tap, or a few clackety-clacks of the keyboard away on a screen. All I'm supposed to do is aggregate the data and—voila!—a tale as old as from 2008 emerges from that tangled web. It's very unlikely that it will ever get archived and relegated to some dumpster in the Ethernet because it's a narrative that will surely be told repeatedly by many generations of hopeful, wannabe tech billionaires to come, inspired by the can-do attitude of the company founders. Kalanick and Camp are like a version of the Wright Brothers for the sharing economy. They broke the rules for what could and couldn't be done when it came to transportation and shook a few other industries to the core. So, check on the easy access to information for telling the story. Told ya my life as an author is simple and trouble-free.

But wait! Because of how widespread the story of Uber has become, especially to the residents of Silicon Valley, it's really quite the headache to figure out a different way of telling it while keeping you, the reader, from zoning out and saying "same old, same old" as you read paragraph after paragraph of the oft-told, dare I say, legend. How is this storytelling going to be any different from what you've already read online?

Well, let me focus on two aspects that make this book distinct: simple is always best, so I'm not going to bog you down with dissertation-worthy outlines so deep that it has as many levels as an underground diamond mine in South Africa. Seven chapters, tops, are what you get from me, with each chapter devoted to a specific aspect of Uber's history. And I'm going to spin this yarn in my own way. Maybe, I'll be irreverent in some sections, but mostly, I'm here just to tell you a damn good narrative of a tech company that earned the creation of a word after its own name. Yes, "uberization" is a real English term now, and it means "the act or process of changing the market for a service by introducing a different way of buying or using it, especially using mobile technology." Not quite canonized yet in either the Merriam-Webster or the Oxford Dictionary, but this definition is already found in the Cambridge Dictionary.[1] Other more jargon-y meanings are available, floating around elsewhere on the Internet—I'm looking at you Wikipedia[2]—but I'm not really interested in telling you about those. It's enough for you to know that uberization is all about changing things up in an industry so that a service becomes far more user-friendly than ever before.

Now, back to this book. So what can you expect from the structure and content of this little opus of mine? For starters, I'll tell you how it all began for Kalanick and Camp in the City of Lights. The first chapter, "Apparently, Paris Isn't Just for Lovers", covers their experience in that European capital, batting at ideas until they hit a home run. It speaks of how the tandem took their concept to various investors and which ones were first to buy into the app and come on board. Yup! Uber is an American company made on French soil. *Oh là là!*

---

[1] *Cambridge Dictionary*, s.v. "uberization (*n.*)," accessed March 11, 2019, https://dictionary.cambridge.org/dictionary/english/uberization.
[2] Wikipedia, s.v. "Uberisation," accessed March 11, 2019, https://en.wikipedia.org/wiki/Uberisation.

The second chapter ("Wreaked Havoc and Got Paid for It") segues into the personal histories of both Travis Kalanick and Garrett Camp. Here, you will discover that despite their seemingly youthful appearance (neither of the two look like they have graduated high school yet), they weren't fresh-faced novices in the entrepreneurial and technological spaces. They were veterans who had battle scars to show off to any interested parties over shots of tequila by the bar. By the time they had gotten together to give birth to Uber, Kalanick and Camp had already earned enough mileage and street cred in Silicon Valley to be worth a keen listen. It was highly unlikely that they would have been turned away by bouncers and bodyguards of billionaires when they started knocking on doors for funds. Their previous experiences had ensured a high rate of success to get their new venture off the ground.

The third chapter ("Answering the Ubiquitous Uber Question of 'Where to?'") is when I truly begin to explore the company's history by focusing on the first steps of Uber into the world as a Transportation Network Company (TNC), from its official 2010 takeoff in San Francisco and on to new grounds like New York City and beyond. The infancy of Uber was definitely not without its perils and threats, especially coming from establishments like the taxi industry, city governments, and the like. Even so, Uber broke through many barriers and made irreversible (most of them anyway) inroads into several more metropolitan areas across the globe.

For the fourth chapter ("The Uncommon Route from Point A to Point B"), I thought it best to feature the various innovations introduced by Uber to the world, as it added more years to its existence. From its flagship, UberBLACK, the company went on to create new services like the UberX and the UberPOOL to cater to as many types of passengers as possible. As expected, there was opposition to pretty much every new offering they served to the general public, but there was no stopping its growth. By then, everybody and their grandmother in any major city definitely paid attention to and knew the company and what it was all about (I may be leaning a bit on the hyperbole there, but you get the idea). "Disruptive" was a common adjective to describe Uber and it certainly was a well-earned badge of honor as it constantly updated its app to make its users' lives just a little less stressed on their regular, holiday, or party commute. However, I'll try to keep the use of the word "disruptive" to a minimum because it's a lazy shorthand for describing the complex process the company and its duo founders undertook in order to pioneer a new way of ferrying people from place to place.

In the fifth chapter ("Even Superhighways Have Cracks, Potholes, and Assholes"), I turn the spotlight on the major scandals that plagued the company from inception to the present day, that is, as of this writing (who knows if there are more brewing in a smoky lair somewhere in the future, you know?). As it made its way to the stratosphere, Uber has had its fair share of turbulence in the form of unsavory business practices, inevitable accidents and crimes, courtroom drama, sexual harassment accusations, and more, which shook the company enough to lead to the main subject matter of the first chapter.

The sixth chapter ("This Is Where the Trip Ends") tells you the events that led to the plummet of Kalanick to earth and his dethronement as CEO of the multibillion-dollar company. Though not a pretty section because blood and gore were spilled on the streets of San Francisco, the experience of Uber's "mega adviser"[3] was, without doubt, a case study of the

---

[3] Maya Kosoff, "A Look Inside the Insanely Successful Life of Billionaire Uber CEO Travis Kalanick," Business Insider, July 6, 2015, https://www.businessinsider.com/inside-the-

pitfalls and downfalls of corporate leadership gone slightly rogue—not precisely textbook, but engaging in a *Schadenfreude* kind of way to outsiders looking in.

Finally, in the seventh chapter ("Life after the Wunderkind Era"), you get a sneak peek into post-Kalanick Uber and its ongoing campaign for world domination. Though still a privately held company as of December 2018, it nevertheless seems destined to do its initial public offering within the next year - 2019.[4] Whether Kalanick's step down healed or harmed the company's prospects for the IPO and other future endeavors very likely divides the audience. I'm sure you have your own thoughts about the matter as I have mine. The important thing to keep in mind though is that there is life after "Travis Kalanick, Uber CEO" for Travis Kalanick and for Uber. Nowadays, the former continues to invest in new ventures and the latter keeps moving people from pickup location to destination every day. And Garrett Camp? He's still the man with a plan, adding

successful-life-of-billionaire-uber-ceo-travis-kalanick-2015-7?IR=T.

[4] Eric Rosenbaum, "Get Ready for the $200 Billion IPO Shakeup in 2019," CNBC, December 17, 2018, https://www.cnbc.com/2018/12/14/get-ready-for-the-200-billion-ipo-shakeup-in-2019.html.

"philanthropy" to his list of accomplishments.[5]

---

[5] Lora Kolodny, "Uber and Infosys Co-founders Are Latest Billionaires to Join the Giving Pledge," CNBC, November 22, 2017, https://www.cnbc.com/2017/11/22/uber-and-infosys-co-founders-join-the-giving-pledge.html.

Chapter 1: Apparently, Paris Isn't Just for Lovers

Paris in winter is just like any other place in the world that experiences a four-season climate year in and year out. The temperatures drop to the point of numbing your soul. Your eyeballs start to feel, paradoxically enough, like the Sahara Desert from the dryness and gritty feel of low humidity, and your skin begs to immerse itself in a tub of shea butter for some relief from the desiccation of its pores. Yes, it's just run-of-the-mill effects of the dreary weather on your frail human frame. Take comfort in the fact that, at least, it's not anywhere near Siberian conditions. Now, that is a different story and requires at least a Laptev Sea-sized supply of vodka.

Meanwhile, the upside to all your suffering is that your backdrop is the Iron Lady herself, standing tall above every other edifice in the *capitale française*.[6] If your joints and muscles must ache and your lips must chap, at least let

---

[6] Stephen Heyman, "Paris Raises Its Silhouette, but Slowly and Not Easily," *New York Times*, June 3, 2015, https://www.nytimes.com/2015/06/04/arts/international/paris-raises-its-silhouette-but-slowly-and-not-easily.html.

them do so under the shadow of the majestic and eternal Eiffel Tower, right? Somehow, its presence makes everything bearable, meaningful, and *très stylé*. Everybody who knows or has heard of Paris could only dream of having an *espresso* and a *croissant* at any of its sidewalk cafés while observing pedestrians wrapped up in their Hermès scarves stride past. But there you are, living out everybody else's fantasy derived from staring for hours at the glossy pages of a *Condé Nast Traveler* thrown carelessly on the coffee table of their globetrotting dentist's office. That's your privilege over them. Of course, said outdoor people-watching rituals happen comfortably only in seasons other than winter, but you get my drift about Paris being this elegant embodiment of *la joie de vivre*.

It was in such a setting—or so I imagined—that the scene was ripe for one of the greatest tech company births of all time. A bit of an exaggeration, perhaps, but I say that because it's not very often that privately owned companies reach unicorn[7] status by being valued at over a billion dollars. And I'm being very conservative about that number. In fact, a

---

[7] James Chen, "Unicorn," Investopedia, December 21, 2017, https://www.investopedia.com/terms/u/unicorn.asp.

team of MIT engineers and Wall Street analysts had examined the valuation of Uber and theorized that it could even be justifiably worth $120 billion.[8] That's $120,000,000,000—that's three commas and a lot of zeros. It's just slightly higher than the 2018 gross domestic product of Puerto Rico, which is estimated at $119,314,000,000 by the International Monetary Fund.[9] It's an economy that relies mainly on agriculture, industry, and services to keep it and over three million people afloat.[10] If you visit the IMF site from which I took Puerto

[8] Trefis Team, "How Uber Could Justify a $120 Billion Valuation," *Forbes*, December 3, 2018, https://www.forbes.com/sites/greatspeculations/2018/12/03/how-uber-could-justify-a-120-billion-valuation/#d8ef0fa7f9b3.

[9] "Report for Selected Countries and Subjects," International Monetary Fund, accessed March 11, 2019, https://www.imf.org/external/pubs/ft/weo/2018/01/weodata/weorept.aspx?pr.x=46&pr.y=12&sy=2018&ey=2018&scsm=1&ssd=1&sort=country&ds=.&br=1&c=512%2C946%2C914%2C137%2C612%2C546%2C614%2C962%2C311%2C674%2C213%2C676%2C911%2C548%2C193%2C556%2C122%2C678%2C912%2C181%2C313%2C867%2C419%2C682%2C513%2C684%2C316%2C273%2C913%2C868%2C124%2C921%2C339%2C948%2C638%2C943%2C514%2C686%2C218%2C688%2C963%2C518%2C616%2C728%2C223%2C836%2C516%2C558%2C918%2C138%2C748%

[10] "Central America: Puerto Rico," CIA World Factbook, accessed March 11, 2019, https://www.cia.gov/library/publications/resources/the-world-factbook/geos/rq.html.

Rico's GDP estimate, you'll see that many other countries registered far shorter digit strings for theirs. Contrast all that to Uber's business model and its human resources. It makes money from a smartphone app that connects would-be passengers with hardworking drivers wanting to churn out more revenue for themselves and to maximize the time they spend on the road. And Uber has only 16,000 employees worldwide to worry about.[11] Mind-boggling and mind-blowing, isn't it?

Now back to Paris in the winter. Unlike the mere mortals that we — you and me – are when given the chance to fly into the Charles de Gaulle Airport, Travis Kalanick and Garrett Camp had a stroll down the Champs-Élysées farthest from their minds that fateful December in 2008.[12] (Or maybe they did, who knows? Point is, I'm trying to tell a story here my way, okay? Besides, well, Kalanick had shown a "romantic" photo of them both standing in front of the Eiffel Tower in a talk before, but that seems to be the only record of them doing

[11] "Facts & Figures," Uber, accessed March 11, 2019, https://www.uber.com/en-KE/newsroom/company-info/.

[12] Avery Hartmans and Nathan McAlone, "The Story of How Travis Kalanick Built Uber into the Most Feared and Valuable Startup in the World," Business Insider, August 1, 2016, https://www.businessinsider.com/ubers-history?IR=T.

anything touristy in that period.[13]) They were both attending LeWeb, one of Europe's largest and longest-running annual technological conferences.[14] As such gatherings go, their minds were preoccupied with all things tech. Most of the time, anyway.

Supposedly after an evening of carousing during the conference,[15] Kalanick and Camp had gone back to the four-bedroom apartment Kalanick had rented to accommodate his friends and himself[16] during the event. Spirits and alcohol levels were probably still high, which is why their behavior was enough to agitate their Parisian taxi driver, who told them off for their rowdiness and threatened to kick

---

[13] Travis Kalanick, "Travis Kalanick at Startup School 2012," October 25, 2013, at Y Combinator Startup School on October 20, 2012 in Stanford Memorial Auditorium, produced by Y Combinator and the Stanford Technology Ventures Program, YouTube video, 28:49, https://www.youtube.com/watch?v=rQ6GoY2_Ujw&t=252s.

[14] "5 Things to Know about LeWeb," LeWebParis, accessed March 11, 2019, https://www.lewebparis.com/things-to-know-about-leweb/.

[15] Mango Research, "How Did Uber Start? The Birth of Travis Kalanick and Garrett Camp's Uber," April 8, 2017, YouTube video, 6:35, https://www.youtube.com/watch?v=wDgCNCd7KzY.

[16] Travis Kalanick, "Travis Kalanick of Uber – TWiST #180," interview by Jason Calacanis, This Week in Startups, August 16 2011, YouTube video, 1:21:38, https://www.youtube.com/watch?v=550X5OZVk7Y&t=99s.

them out of his vehicle. Angered by the driver's own rudeness, Kalanick jumped out of the cab and Camp followed, together with Melody McCloskey, a television producer and Camp's former girlfriend and good friend. It was just another bad experience to add to the many woes both he and Camp had experienced in the hands of cabbies and the taxi industry as a whole. That incident may have also finally drawn Kalanick to the table to discuss the possibility of the new company Camp had been talking about all throughout the conference.[17]

Prior to that incident, they had already been testing various ideas for new companies with friends and each other. While Kalanick was focused on creating something similar to Airbnb, which he called Pad Pass, Camp stuck to his guns on inventing an app that could make rides accessible to people at the simple touch of a button. He envisioned owning a fleet of luxury cars to rival the ever-present black Lincolns that embodied traveling in style, especially within an urban setting. He wanted this service to be available to his friends and himself on demand. In turn, as users, they were to pay for the privilege to ride in them and to cover costs like parking. Kalanick listened to his friend but

[17] Mango, "How Did Uber Start?"

wasn't really keen on it, possibly until that irate Parisian cabbie moment.

Camp had been residing in San Francisco since StumbleUpon, the very first tech company he founded together with Geoff Smith in 2001, moved to the home of the Golden Gate Bridge. He had a regular dose of difficult cabbies because it was a constant struggle for him to hail a cab to go from place to place at the time that he needed it.[18] Imagine that happening to a guy who owned a Mercedes Benz C-Class but couldn't even drive it around the hilly and windy roads of the city because it was a magnet for a potential break-in. The stress of a basic logistical headache: looking for safe parking for such a fancy sports car, was just not worth all that trouble in the crazily planned San Francisco city layout.

Let me pause here for a minute and acknowledge the fact that there actually seems to be various versions of the origin story of Uber, even coming from both protagonists, Kalanick and Camp themselves. I've watched enough videos of interviews and lectures and

---

[18] Brad Stone, "Uber: The App That Changed How the World Hails a Taxi," *Guardian*, January 29, 2017, https://www.theguardian.com/technology/2017/jan/29/uber-app-changed-how-world-hails-a-taxi-brad-stone/.

read more than my fair share of articles to know this to be true. I can even throw you the little anecdote about Camp being inspired in part by Daniel Craig's first outing as James Bond in *Casino Royale*. He was captivated by the scene of Bond tracking another car's movements from his phone, regardless of how far behind he was trailing. It was a visual that Camp aspired his own app to have. He wanted users to see how close their ride was to their waiting point in real time[19] (it's this very feature of the app that I personally appreciate because, say, in inclement weather, it's not going to be rocket science for me to figure out when I'm supposed to step out into the rain to get into my Uber. I just need to see its icon right next to my pin on the screen to know that it has already arrived).

So yes, there seems to be various versions of the company's origins, but the fundamentals of the story remain the same. As with all great inventions, Uber was created because there was an unmet need, a persistent unsolved problem that was begging to be fixed. For sure, many major cities suffer from it: at certain times of the day, at certain points of their road systems, it was nearly impossible to grab a cab, even if the future of Planet Earth depended on it or the

---

[19] Stone, "Uber."

zombie apocalypse had arrived and you needed to get to safety. When you're rushing to catch a flight or trying not to be late for the job interview of your life, this situation was simply untenable.

By the time Camp came head to head with the taxi industry status quo, he was already a very rich man, enjoying the fruits of his labor after eBay had bought StumbleUpon, "a social network that helps you discover unique and interesting things across the Web . . . a discovery engine of entertainment that recommends photography, art, humor, fashion, sports, technology and just about every other topic you can think of,"[20] for a whopping (at that time) $75 million. Not bad an accomplishment for a then 28-year-old dude. How do you think he was able to afford a snobbishly expensive sports car? But the thing about Camp was that he was not really the type to drive or a snob. In Canada, where he was born and raised, he took public transport most of the time, so the situation in San Francisco was a frustration for him, compounded when he had to go on dates and

[20] DashBurst, "What Is StumbleUpon and How Does It Work?" Small Business Trends, updated February 9, 2019, https://smallbiztrends.com/2014/08/what-is-stumbleupon-how-do-i-use-it.html.

had way too many late entrances.[21] He wasn't trying to be that kind of a jerk.

If there's anything that I've learned from researching about Camp it's that he's a very tenacious person. Once he latches onto a problem, he doesn't let go until he finds a solution to it, just like all the great innovators throughout history. So there he was, digging deep into the limitations of the transport industry in San Francisco, which he could easily—and correctly, too—infer as the state of affairs in other metropolitan areas.

It's now a bit comical to think that Uber came about because there was a Canadian multimillionaire living in the United States of America, who couldn't have his way with his preferred mode of transportation. But that's exactly what seemed to have happened. Camp didn't like the experience of being stranded on the streets of San Francisco one too many times.[22] And that wasn't him being an entitled boor of a man. His weariness about the whole situation was certainly shared by many other

---

[21] Stone, "Uber."

[22] Garrett Camp, "How I Came Up with Uber – The Startup Mentality with Garrett Camp – Zeitgeist 2016," interview, Zeitgeist Minds, September 23, 2016, YouTube video, 12:48, https://www.youtube.com/watch?v=_vxk4Z1u7RE.

people, but he was hell-bent on the best solution for himself first. He may never have said it in public in these exact words, but I'm pretty sure he was his first user in mind.

Something I've observed about the very best human innovations in history is that when they're created from the pioneers' deep sense of personal need, there's true ownership in the enterprise and it results in something genuinely amazing and life-changing. I'm sure that when the wheel was first invented by some anonymous person or persons from some unknown culture (no one culture can be correctly credited for its invention[23]), it wasn't a fanciful toy to play with. It offered a real utility to humans of the early days. It was no joke hauling boulders and materials across unfriendly geographies yet to be tamed and brought into the confines of developed civilizations. That's just way too much of a dose of backbreaking toil for both humans and their chosen beasts of burden.

It was a good thing that Camp was no longer fully involved in the daily operations of StumbleUpon (eBay acquisition, remember?)

---

[23] "Mankind's Greatest Inventions," History, accessed March 11, 2019, https://www.history.co.uk/shows/mankind-the-story-of-all-of-us/articles/mankinds-greatest-inventions.

because it gave him a lot of leeway to work on his brand-new idea. So what was the relevant information he needed to know about the taxi industry in San Francisco, which would have a direct bearing on his next steps? The city had a cap on the number of taxi licenses it issued: 1,500. The law of supply and demand covering taxis was absolutely nuts. While the drivers experienced a lot of dead time because there were simply no passengers needing their services at certain hours of the day, there were commuters who were ready to pull their hair out by the roots because they were being ignored by empty cabs passing by.[24] There had to be a way of calibrating those two frequent occurrences for a seamless, headache-free experience for both parties.

Even while Camp continued to gather information on the industry he was about to shake up, he was also meeting with other entrepreneurial and tech people like him Nothing like iron sharpening iron right there. After all, teamwork is really the name of the game when you want to go far in your endeavors. One of the very first people who heard about Camp's plan was Tim Ferriss, an American author and investor from New York,

---

[24] Stone, "Uber."

whom he brainstormed with in the early part of 2008 at a bar in the Mission District.[25] A follow-up phone call of that discussion over drinks didn't happen until a couple of months later and Ferriss was clearly impressed at the depth of Camp's progress on research and the increase of his resolve to address the deep-seated problems in the taxi industry. There was also Oscar Salazar, Camp's friend from graduate school at the University of Calgary and an accomplished engineer, whom Camp visited on his way to LeWeb that year,[26] even prior to meeting up with Kalanick in Paris. It was Salazar who was tasked to develop the app prototype. Although he couldn't then receive any cold-hard cash for his efforts being a Mexican on an American student visa, which restricted his ability to work for pay, the equity he was given at that time is now worth nine figures.

And, of course, Camp had also bounced off his idea on McCloskey herself, when they were still dating. Although she was herself an admirer of his creativity, she had her doubts about Uber and expressed it to him.[27] Nonetheless, it didn't slow down Camp's planning. All throughout

---

[25] *Ibid.*
[26] Stone, "Uber."
[27] *Ibid.*

2008, he played around with the right name for his new initiative until he settled on UberCab, whose domain name he registered in August of that year. Then in November, he created a limited liability company for it, just a month before LeWeb.[28] The stage was set so that by the time he met up with Kalanick in the City of Lights, it was just a matter of him lassoing in Kalanick to complete the trinity together with Salazar. Paris was the point of convergence for all the necessary elements to make Uber a reality.

From Kalanick's perspective, however, the LeWeb get-together was when the idea for Uber was hammered out,[29] completely ignoring the groundwork made by Camp and making it confusing for us outsiders to figure out what really went down in those very critical months leading up to the official founding of the company in March 2009.[30] From what I could piece together from various sources, especially from a Kalanick interview by Jason Calacanis, an eventual seed-round investor of Uber, important refinements to the service were brought in by Kalanick in Paris, for sure.[31]

---

[28] *Ibid.*

[29] *Ibid.*

[30] Hartmans and McAlone, "Story."

[31] Kalanick, "TWiST."

Foremost among those contributions, Calacanis was telling Camp that Uber shouldn't own any of the assets, such as the luxury cars and a parking lease. While Camp did push back a bit on Kalanick's suggestion, he eventually accepted it and, to this day, it remains a cornerstone to the business model of Uber. They supply the app for a fee and work the back office needed to support Uber.

Kalanick claimed that, while Camp brought an elegance to the Uber service, it was he who established the mathematical efficiency of their company.[32] Regardless of the details involved in whose origin story, what is important and abundantly clear is that, at the end of 2008 and moving into 2009, Uber was now that much closer to gracing phone screens, with everybody's ideas finding usefulness in various aspects of its functionality. No owned assets, as Kalanick stressed. Real-time tracking, as imagined by Camp. Yup! It was a good and complementary partnership. And to Kalanick's credit, he was always clear that Camp was the true father of the Uber concept,[33] even if he

---

[32] *Ibid.*

[33] Alyson Shontell, "All Hail the Uber Man! How Sharp-Elbowed Salesman Travis Kalanick Became Silicon Valley's Newest Star," Business Insider, January 11, 2014,

himself became the more prominent face of the company as CEO, after acting first as the "chief incubator" or "mega advisor" in 2009.[34] And that was how they spent their first year as a company: a lot of testing, a lot of incubating, and a lot of tweaking. There was real diligence in how they obtained proof of concept for their service. That was their astuteness born of previous experience at work.

At launch in 2010, UberCab (Uber's original name) provided this fundamental service: users could request and pay for a ride by tapping a button on the app or sending a text message, which would then communicate their pickup locations to drivers close by. While it was one and a half times more expensive than a regular San Francisco taxi (after all, its initial conception was to be a rival to black-car services), it was an instant hit among Bay Area people who had downloaded the app onto their phones. Even though costlier than a regular cab, Uber was still much more reasonably priced than a Lincoln. The convenience, affordability, and accessibility of rides were meant to give them a feeling of the baller life and to put it

https://www.businessinsider.com/uber-travis-kalanick-bio-2014-1?IR=T.
[34] Shontell, "Hail."

within their reach.[35] Even Ryan Graves, Uber's first CEO albeit briefly, mentioned as much in an early Uber blog post.[36] Yup! Live the life of a baller in an Uber.

Since then, UberCab has evolved into Uber and become so much more than just a ride-hailing service. With its forays into food delivery, self-driving cars, and on-demand temporary staffing,[37] it has become a behemoth of a logistics company. And there is no stopping its expansion into other industries any time soon for as long as it has some of the most brilliant innovators on its team.

By 2010, Uber wasn't going out into the world on its own, fueled only by the ramen most techies survived on in the startup stage of their companies. It was in need of investments. Perhaps because both Kalanick and Camp were no strangers to Silicon Valley, they garnered interest from key personalities.

During its seed-funding round, Uber had 32 investors, including First Round Capital and

---

[35] Kalanick, "TWiST."

[36] Shontell, "Hail."

[37] Sean O'Kane, "Uber Is Testing an On-demand Staffing Business Called Uber Works," Verge, October 18, 2018, https://www.theverge.com/2018/10/18/17995398/uber-works-staffing-business-test-trial.

other venture capital firms like Founder Collective, Lowercase Capital, and Kapor Capital.[38] A more detailed (read: narrative) source described that in the summer of 2010, Jason Calacanis (brought up earlier), a startup investor and entrepreneur, had organized an Open Angel Forum to highlight then UberCab's need to raise $1 million in investments at a $4 million pre-money valuation.[39] Calacanis himself was first to jump on the bandwagon followed by Chris Falic, who represented First Round Capital. Chris Sacca of Lowercase Capital was in as well and so was Shawn Fanning, who was Kalanick's former competitor, when the latter was still involved with Scour (a little more about Fanning and the competition he brought to Kalanick's previous venture in the next chapter). From that event, Uber was able to raise $1.25 million to fuel its operations and give it its much-needed push forward.

By the time the seed round happened, Uber was already running under the leadership of Ryan Graves. As all stories of great companies go,

---

[38] Becky Peterson, "7 People You Never Realized Were Early Investors in Uber," Business Insider by Pulse, December 30, 2018, https://www.pulse.com.gh/bi/tech/7-people-you-never-realized-were-early-investors-in-uber/9n6z1c8.
[39] Shontell, "Hail."

Graves's recruitment was the stuff of legends. On January 5, 2010, Kalanick had tweeted (verbatim, unedited):

Looking 4 entrepreneurial product mgr/biz-dev killer 4 a location based service.. pre-launch, BIG equity, big peeps involved--ANY TIPS??

Three minutes later, Graves replied (also verbatim and unedited):

@KonaTbone heres a tip. email me :) graves.ryan[at]gmail.com.[40]

Later in the night, they had a two-hour conversation, which lasted past midnight. Presumably, that was Graves's job interview. A month later, in February 2010,[41] Graves moved to San Francisco and became the general manager and CEO of a rather motley crew that shared similar unusual recruitment experiences. Uber was well underway.

---

[40] Hartmans and McAlone, "Story."

[41] Adam Lashinsky, "Uber: An Oral History," *Fortune*, June 3, 2015, http://fortune.com/2015/06/03/uber-an-oral-history/.

Chapter 2: Wreaking Havoc to the Status Quo and Getting Paid for It

Before I continue with the story of Uber, I think it is well worth devoting a bit of time to knowing the individual histories of its founders, Travis Kalanick and Garrett Camp. The mission and vision (and everything else that follows) of a company are often reflective of the character and passion of its founders and that is true even of Uber. In fact, it's not just the grand ideas that the founders' personalities affect; it's also the office culture. It's very important to remember this because of what I'll be narrating to you later.

Anyway, so a way of understanding a bit of the birth and growth of the company is to put a magnifying glass to the tandem and see what may or may not have influenced the many twists and turns of their lives that led to the creation of Uber. Since I had given more airtime to Camp in the previous chapter, let me start off this one by telling Kalanick's story first and then moving on to Camp's.

Travis Kalanick: The Serial Entrepreneur

Kalanick did not begin his first business in the tech world. It was as analog as businesses went. He ran an SAT prep service where, as a teacher, he offered a course that ensured high test scores for its learners. He was funded in part by the father of one of his students, a Korean who recruited clients, that is, parents of potential SAT learners from his home church.[42] Kalanick's own SAT score was a high 1580 and that solidified his credentials and credibility as a tutor. He achieved this when he was only 18 years old.[43]

Because of his self-confessed proficiency in mathematics, it wasn't a surprise when Kalanick went on to study Computer Engineering at the University of California, Los Angeles.[44] It was there where he met the founders of Scour Inc., a company that provided Scour Exchange, a peer-to-peer search engine for files, videos, movies, and images.[45] Five

---

[42] Kalanick, "TWiST."

[43] Shontell, "Hail."

[44] *Britannica*, s.v. "Travis Kalanick," accessed March 11, 2019, https://www.britannica.com/biography/Travis-Kalanick.

[45] Maya Kosoff, "Travis Kalanick's First Company Got Sued for $250 Billion—So He Started a New Revenge Business That Made Him a Millionaire," Business Insider, September 8,

students from the UCLA Computer Science Department (Vince Busam, Michael Todd, Dan Rodrigues, Jason Droege, and Kevin Smilak) were responsible for creating the service in December 1997. In mid-1998, Kalanick, together with Ilya Haykinson, went on to join forces with them as fellow Computer Science students.[46] A year later, Michael Ovitz, former president of Walt Disney Company, and Richard Wolpert, former Disney Online executive, together with Ron Burkle, another investor, acquired a 51 percent stake in the company. By the time of the buy-in, Scour was already enjoying 1.5 million page views daily,[47] which was a stratospheric Internet statistic in those days.

When interviewed about their investment decision, Wolpert explained, "A large portion of Scour's user base comes from @Home [a high-speed cable ISP that operated from 1996 until

---

2015, https://www.businessinsider.com/travis-kalanicks-first-company-got-sued-for-250-billion-so-he-started-a-new-revenge-business-that-made-him-a-millionaire-2015-9?IR=T.
[46] Wikipedia, s.v. "Scour Inc.," accessed March 11, 2019, https://en.wikipedia.org/wiki/Scour_Inc.
[47] Marc Graser, "Ovitz Adds Scour to Online Portfolio," *Variety*, June 11, 1999, https://variety.com/1999/digital/news/ovitz-adds-scour-to-online-portfolio-1117502994/.

2002, when it filed for bankruptcy[48]], which clearly shows that Scour's users are embracing the broadband movement and using Scour for their online access to digital media. And this is the perfect fit with our strategy to help build strong Internet and entertainment companies on the Web."[49] The irony was deep in Wolpert's words vis-à-vis the eventual downfall of @Home a mere three years later, which he certainly wouldn't have predicted. However, Ovitz and Wolpert were not wrong in seeing the important role the Internet had to play in the future of entertainment, primarily in video and audio streaming. What's on the buffet table? Netflix, Amazon Prime Video, Hulu, Spotify, and Pandora are just five of countless examples of online entertainment currently available. Other countries would have their own versions of such services.

I mention the Ovitz investment to give you an idea as to how significant the Scour multimedia search engine was at that time. A powerful Hollywood mogul like Ovitz and Burkle, a supermarket magnate, had actually paid $4 million for the controlling interest of the

---

[48] Wikipedia, s.v. "@Home Network," accessed March 11, 2019, https://en.wikipedia.org/wiki/@Home_Network.
[49] Graser, "Ovitz."

relatively young company.[50] This should also explain why Kalanick may have dropped out of UCLA to devote his time fully to Scour Inc. A company that could fetch that price in its fledgling state was a company worth giving up a college diploma for—or so it seemed. It was a sacrifice he appeared willing to take and he was certainly relentless in fulfilling his role as the marketing and business development guy of the bunch. In a controversial move to market Scour Exchange, Kalanick had shortened the name to SX. He then hired a third-party marketing company to hang lubricants on the doors of dorm rooms, together with hang tags and stickers that announced, "Do not enter, SX going on."[51] What was very clear in those early years of Kalanick's entrepreneurial life was that he truly knew how to tell a damn good story to push his product or service.

That's really one thing you need to remember about entrepreneurship these days, especially if you're hoping to follow in Kalanick's footsteps. You should be able to put together a compelling

---

[50] Chris Raymond, "Travis Kalanick: 'You Can Either Do What They Say or You Can Fight for What You Believe," Success, February 13, 2017, https://www.success.com/travis-kalanick-you-can-either-do-what-they-say-or-you-can-fight-for-what-you-believe/.
[51] Shontell, "Hail."

narrative that would engage your audience, get them to act upon something. People today love gathering around a cause and a well-told cause is likely to draw people to it like ants to a picnic basket filled with chocolate and fruit. So whether you're merely a wannabe Instagram influencer aiming to be a brand ambassador of, say, Urban Outfitters, or headed towards the rarefied heights of the Oprahs and Obamas of the world, you better be the best damn storyteller in your neighborhood.

When you hear Kalanick tell the story of what happened next between Ovitz and Scour, you'd really be drawn to the whole cloak-and-dagger drama of it all. In a nutshell, Ovitz's agreement with Scour included a clause that prevented the company from looking for other investors, giving preferential treatment to Ovitz and Burkle to buy more equity shares within a specified time. When that period was about to run out and the Scour team asked their first investors for their move ("May we go ahead and shop our company to other people, pretty please?"), Ovitz sued the company to preempt any shopping. Essentially, Ovitz was asking the court to compel the UCLA kids to take his money.[52]

Later on, when Kalanick had a chance to give a public talk, one of Ovitz's henchmen was there to deliver a cryptic message (whispered into Kalanick's ear from behind him), which translated to something like "under no circumstance was he to smear the good reputation of the Hollywood czar in his speech because Ovitz had worked so many years to build it up." The incident appeared to have visibly shaken him when he finally went on stage, as Calacanis observed.[53] Since then, Ovitz and Kalanick appeared to have clarified the incident to each other. It is no longer an issue or a contribution to bad blood between them. Just the same, it was a well-spun Kalanick tale worthy of mention.

Two years after Scour started, well, scouring IP addresses for multimedia files to keep its users happy, a new kid in the form of Napster came on the block, pitting them both against each other for lordship over the search-engine space. While they had similar objectives, there were a few distinct differences between the two, one of which was that Napster dealt only with music. Scour, on the other hand, did music plus videos

---

[52] Kalanick, "TWiST."
[53] Ibid.

and more. Napster kept to community hard drives for the "where" of their searches. Scour cast out a broader net to include the whole wide Web.[54] An interesting discovery for me was that Shawn Fanning, Napster co-founder (and whom I had mentioned in the previous chapter as a seed investor of Uber), was himself one of the early users of Scour.[55] Considering how these tech geeks work, I wouldn't be surprised if Napster was partly inspired by what Fanning experienced as he used the first multimedia search engine. I mean, that's really how technology grows, right? Each new iteration is supposed to be an improvement, a lovechild, or a solution of something previously made. Sadly, both suffered from the same ignominious bullying by the combined forces of the entertainment industry.

If anything, the real war was not Ovitz versus Scour but the film and music industries versus Scour. The search engine was very popular among its users because it gave them access to multimedia content free and that did not sit well with the movie studios and record labels. They were not about to tolerate the copyright

[54] Damien Cave, "Why Scour Is Not the New Napster," Salon, August 22, 2000, https://www.salon.com/2000/08/22/scour/
[55] Kosoff, "Travis."

infringement to their intellectual properties, so they sued Scour for $250 billion[56]—or as Kalanick, the stellar storyteller put it, "a quarter of a trillion dollars"[57] because trillion does sound more impressive than billion. The lawsuit very quickly forced Scour to file for Chapter 11, rendering the litigation moot. Certainly, the entertainment people were not thrilled that their case was going to be settled in a bankruptcy court. That was just way too anticlimactic, like Thelma and Louise deciding to surrender peacefully to the law enforcers hot on their tail.

I'm pretty sure that neither Kalanick nor other Scour personnel wanted things to end that way either, so Kalanick pulled off a very Kalanick move. He conceptualized a new company born from the rubble of Scour in 2001. In a scheme to exact revenge from the 33 Scour litigants and to make them pay (literally, as his future customers),[58] together with Todd, one of the Scour founding five, Kalanick created Red Swoosh. Red Swoosh was a "peer-to-peer content delivery company that develops client-side technology to support, manage, and

[56] *Ibid.*
[57] Kalanick, "TWiST."
[58] Shontell, "Hail."

distribute media files."[59] In other words, it created a program or system, which allows you to access multimedia content legally, and to organize and play it.

Among the early investors of Kalanick's new business was Mark Cuban, best known for his role as billionaire investor on the multi-awarded reality TV show, *Shark Tank* (Cuban himself got his first couple of millions from technology, selling MicroSolutions, a system integrator and software reseller he established, to CompuServe[60]). That was in spite of the fact that Cuban and Kalanick had had some very public online disagreements,[61] which were really not unusual between a pair of smart and very assertive techies used to having their own respective way. Cuban having Kalanick's back is reminiscent of Fanning investing early on in Uber. I guess, when these guys find something elegant and profitable, it doesn't really matter that they've had their disputes and competitions. Investments in technology are about the now and the future. The past is best

[59] *Crunchbase*, s.v. "Red Swoosh," accessed March 11, 2019, https://www.crunchbase.com/organization/red-swoosh#section-overview.
[60] *Wikipedia*, s.v. "Mark Cuban," accessed March 11, 2019, https://en.wikipedia.org/wiki/Mark_Cuban.
[61] Kalanick, "TWiST."

archived.

Unsurprisingly (because of the burgeoning trend of the Web then as a portal to multimedia content), it took only six years before Red Swoosh was bought by Akamai Technologies, a "content delivery network and cloud service provider headquartered in Cambridge, Massachusetts,"[62] for about $19 million. The acquisition came right on time, when the company was beginning to run low on funds.[63] The deal made Kalanick an instant multimillionaire and gave him a chance to recover from his Scour and Red Swoosh burnout phase and to travel around the world for a bit.

While the Red Swoosh deal that made him a millionaire was a highlight of Kalanick's entrepreneurial journey thus far, the truth was that the internal workings of the company were not really very kosher, which explained and legitimized his claim of exhaustion.[64] Prior to its acquisition, the company was constantly plagued by cash-flow issues, regular disagreements with Todd, and difficulties in

[62] *Wikipedia*, s.v. "Akamai Technologies," accessed March 11, 2019, https://en.wikipedia.org/wiki/Akamai_Technologies.
[63] Kosoff, "Travis."
[64] Shontell, "Hail."

getting investor interest in a "software" in the post-9/11 economic scenario. Kalanick needed distance between the tech world and himself to breathe again and to get back his bearings. And let's be honest, he probably wanted girls again in his life because living in his mother's house to save money was seriously cramping his style, based on how he described his situation then during an interview. He was done with his ramen time.[65]

And it was in that space that Camp stumbled upon him, sprawled out on the ground in utter exhaustion and not really interested in making a new commitment to another startup. At least, not yet. Not until Kalanick fully understood the profound ramifications of what Camp was proposing to him.

Garrett Camp: The Creator of Life-Changing Services

In the early days of Uber, Garrett Camp was not as much in the limelight as Kalanick was, at least that's the impression I got when I tried to read up on him. He wasn't as talked about or prominently featured by the media as Kalanick was. Everybody knew him as the co-founder of

---

[65] Kalanick, "TWiST."

Uber, but compared to Kalanick, he was a bit low key, probably choosing instead to toil in the background away from the eye of the voyeuristic public. When I googled for his bio, there weren't as many available online as Kalanick's.

As I had mentioned in the previous chapter, Camp was born in Canada and raised in Calgary, where he was introduced early on to personal computers, thanks to an uncle who had gifted his family a Macintosh.[66] From that point on, it seemed like Camp was hooked to the machine and all things tech, and he spent a lot of time learning how it worked and what he could make it do.

Similar to Kalanick's college plan when he didn't travel outside his home state of California, Camp's own plan led him to the University of Calgary, which was still well within his backyard, so to speak. Camp had no real reason to move far away from his parents' cozy house, at least not until he finished his undergraduate diploma in electrical engineering and carried on to take up his Master of Science degree. It was then that he moved to a campus apartment.[67]

---

[66] Stone, "Uber."

[67] *Ibid*.

Camp came to be friends with Geoff Smith at the university through a childhood friend. They obviously shared common interests because they soon banded together to create StumbleUpon in 2001. It was a search engine of sorts designed to help people discover sites more aligned to their interests.[68] Perhaps a comparable (not exactly the same, okay?) experience to what it did is what happens these days, say, on a site like Netflix. Its algorithm notes the TV shows and movies you "thumb up" versus the ones you "thumb down" and lines up appropriate suggestions to you for your future viewing (in the case of StumbleUpon, the suggestions it gave you could also be influenced by other people's votes). It looks like so many other sites and apps have that type of feature configured into their code nowadays (*cough* Facebook *cough*) as standard functionality because the big data they gather from it is especially very useful for them when their primary revenues come from advertising. They like being able to identify targeted audiences for their advertisers. The latter feel it's a worthwhile spend for their companies.

It didn't take long for StumbleUpon to gain wide

[68] "Garrett Camp," What Success, accessed March 11, 2019, http://whatsuccess.com/success-story-garrett-camp/.

popularity that attracted the attention of Brad O'Neill, a Silicon Valley investor, who gave funds to grow the rookie company and suggested its relocation to San Francisco.[69] Camp moved to the city along with his company, which pretty much exposed him to countless taxi woes that propelled him to create Uber. But before that momentous event happened, there was another that came first in 2007. That year, StumbleUpon was acquired by eBay for $75 million,[70] which thrust Camp into the exclusive club of rich techies and celebrated the company as one of the early successes of Web 2.0, "the movement in which companies such as Flickr and Facebook mined the social connections among internet users,"[71] which is geek-speak for the Web moving from merely being a portal for knowledge and information to being a portal for a new and different level of social interactions, engagements, and relationships (at present, the extreme manifestation of that would be people establishing their worth as human beings from

---

[69] *Wikipedia*, s.v. "StumbleUpon," accessed March 11, 2019, https://en.wikipedia.org/wiki/StumbleUpon.
[70] "eBay's StumbleUpon Acquisition: Confirmed at $75 Million," TechCrunch, accessed March 11, 2019, https://techcrunch.com/2007/05/30/ebays-stumbleupon-acquisition-confirmed-at-75-million/.
[71] Stone, "Uber."

the number of likes they can get from a single post. Staggering, isn't it?). Within 10 years of inception, StumbleUpon supposedly boasted 25 million registered users.[72]

Unlike Kalanick's entrepreneurial journey, which was fraught with a good number of controversies, Camp's was generally quiet and on an even keel. Camp didn't have to deal with any lawsuits or death threats towards him. Neither he nor his company had to file a Chapter 11 to save their asses. Perhaps, the only moment that could have rocked the boat for Camp was when eBay decided to resell StumbleUpon two short years after its acquisition, in 2009.[73] Reading between the lines of a press release issued by StumbleUpon, it appeared as though they had gone back to square one in terms of their funding status ("returned to the ranks of an investor-backed startup"[74]) and that there wasn't really any

[72] What Success, "Camp."

[73] Dan Frommer, "eBay Dumps StumbleUpon," Business Insider, April 13, 2009, https://www.businessinsider.com/ebay-lets-go-of-stumbleupon-2009-4?IR=T.

[74] Kara Swisher, "StumbleUpon Stumbles Out of eBay's Arms to Be Reborn as a Startup (Plus the Entire Press Release)," All Things Digital, April 13, 2009, http://allthingsd.com/20090413/stumbleupon-stumbles-out-of-ebays-arms-to-be-reborn-as-a-start-up/.

common ground for the respective visions and goals of eBay and StumbleUpon to come together and turn a profit (very important for enterprises) for them both ("there were few long-term synergies between the two businesses"[75]).

Thankfully (from the perspective of the rank and file, for sure), Camp and other former StumbleUpon investors were quick to snap it up again. The company's operations carried on for 16 years from its founding year until it was shut down for good in 2018, with all StumbleUpon accounts migrating to Mix, another discovery service platform similar to it but with more features.[76] And guess what? Mix is actually a project under Expa, a "startup studio" founded by Camp, which develops and launches new and successful companies.[77] In simple terms, Expa sounds very much like an incubator with the added value of being backed by Camp's and his partners' years of experience.

[75] *Ibid*.
[76] Antonio Villas-Boas, "StumbleUpon, the Addictive Internet Tool Made by an Uber Cofounder Who Brought You to Random Sites, Is Folding," Business Insider, May 24, 2018, https://www.businessinsider.com/stumbleupon-is-shutting-down-2018-5?IR=T.
[77] "About," Expa, accessed March 11, 2019, https://www.expa.com/#about.

As with StumbleUpon and Uber, Mix is a product that addresses Camp's forever questing mind; it is something that he himself wants in his life.[78] Mix is a refinement of StumbleUpon in that it factors in the value of social networks into the equation of content curation. Don't forget that at the time StumbleUpon was launched, social networks were barely in existence.[79] As Camp himself explained, "Mix.com combines social and semantic personalization into one streamlined experience. It also makes it easier for people to organize content into meaningful collections. This will help you find obscure but interesting content that has been recommended by people you know and trust."[80] Clearly, Camp is a visionary who looks way into the future.

Something very interesting about both Kalanick

---

[78] Jordan Crook, "Garrett Camp's Latest Expa Project, Mix, Aims to Curate the Web," TechCrunch, accessed March 11, 2019, https://techcrunch.com/2017/08/01/garrett-camps-latest-expa-project-mix-aims-to-curate-the-web/.

[79] Biz Carson, "Uber Cofounder Garrett Camp Is Back to an Old Problem: Finding Interesting Things on the Internet," Forbes, August 1, 2018, https://www.forbes.com/sites/bizcarson/2018/08/01/uber-cofounder-garrett-camp-is-back-to-an-old-problem-finding-interesting-things-on-the-internet/#3e8e58a26c9d.

[80] Garrett Camp, "SU Is Moving to Mix," Medium, May 23, 2018, https://medium.com/@gc/su-is-moving-to-mix-c2c3bff037a5.

and Camp: while their new wealth afforded them luxuries (for example, Kalanick's Jam Pad[81] and Camp's Mercedes Benz), they never stopped looking out for the next big idea out there. Red Swoosh and StumbleUpon were just the beginning. Their minds were constantly churning out innovative concepts and solving problems. Their eyes were ceaselessly on the lookout for a new project, a new business to incubate and to launch. All those were essential and great character traits to have because they brought Kalanick and Camp together to collaborate on one of the greatest tech successes of all time to date, not just in terms of valuation but in terms of spread, impact, and collective innovations.

---

[81] Lyanne Alfaro, "Uber's CEO Used to Host Intimate Jam Sessions at His Home So Entrepreneurs Could Hash Out Business Ideas," Business Insider, September 8, 2015, https://www.businessinsider.com/uber-ceo-hosted-jam-sessions-at-his-home-for-entrepreneurs-to-hash-out-business-ideas-2015-9?IR=T.

Chapter 3: Answering the Ubiquitous Uber Question of "Where to?"

Nowadays, when you open the Uber app, the first thing you see is the question, "Where to?" Then you have to input your destination on the screen, so it can give you a choice of ride types available, their respective fares, and the estimated time of arrival to your drop-off point. The new screen will also show you the suggested route on the map, how many Uber drivers are in your general vicinity, and how many minutes away the nearest available driver is. All that data makes for sensible navigation of the app and for fairly reliable logistical planning.

And that is what Uber has become now: a company in the business of making logistics a little easier for all of us. If you've ever experienced the frustration of hailing a yellow cab in Manhattan on a Friday night to get to your best friend's wedding reception at the Boathouse in Central Park, with brief stops at Tribeca for the wedding cake from Baked on Church Street and at NoHo for a case of cabernet sauvignon from Astor Wines and Spirits on Lafayette Street, then you know that

Uber changed the game completely and has made that exasperating scenario (almost) a thing of the past. The heartache from being ignored by an empty taxi passing in front of you is no longer a thing. Everything can now be negotiated and set firmly with a few swipes, jabs, and scrolls on your Samsung Galaxy Note 10. Or—I won't judge—your iPhone X.

But mind you: Uber didn't get to this level of competence and efficiency without experiencing its fair share of highs and lows since its establishment in 2010. Certainly, just like many other enterprises, it had a Ph.D.'s worth of lessons to learn along the way.

As you know by now, Uber set up its headquarters in San Francisco and had its official launch in the same city, offering nothing but black-car service at that time, under its original name, UberCab. It proved to be a big hit among its first users in the Bay Area, but just a few months later, in October 2010, it received a cease-and-desist letter from the San Francisco Metro Transit Authority and the Public Utilities Commission of California, regarding its operations. The big concerns for the said institutions were that UberCab was not in compliance with some of their regulations. The company was ready with a response: "UberCab is a first-to-market, cutting-edge transportation technology and it must be recognized that the regulations from both city and state regulatory bodies have not been written with these innovations in mind. As such, we are happy to help educate the regulatory bodies on this new generation of technology and work closely with both agencies to ensure compliance and keep our service available for our true Uber users and their drivers."[82]

This was the first shot of resistance fired, which set the tone for much of the timeline progression of Uber. It was constantly in conflict, deliberately or not, with deeply entrenched institutions in society that, as is expected of humans, were against the notion of change and constant flux. In this case, in order to address the primary issue raised that it was operating as a taxi business without the required documentation and licenses, UberCab dropped the second part of its name to avoid any ambiguity and became just Uber from that point on.[83] It positioned itself outside the box in

[82] Lora Kolodny, "UberCab Ordered to Cease and Desist," TechCrunch, accessed March 11, 2019, https://techcrunch.com/2010/10/24/ubercab-ordered-to-cease-and-desist/.
[83] *Id*., "UberCab, Now Just Uber, Shares Cease-and-Desist Orders," TechCrunch, accessed March 11, 2019,

which they were lumped up together with the rest of the taxi and limousine industries.

In hindsight, the name change was probably the best thing they could have done because this kicked the door wide open for the business to be so much more than just a ride-hailing service. Years later, it allowed Uber to explore other industries where it could shake up the status quo. You know . . . uberize them. It was a brilliant branding move if you ask me.

I am theorizing that the San Francisco skirmish awakened the company to this reality: they could expect to run up against various oppositions every step of the way. In that case, perhaps they needed someone at the helm of the company, who had firsthand experience of David-versus-Goliath scenarios. Later that same year, in December 2010, a major power shuffle happened. Thankfully, it wasn't anything dramatic; both parties involved confirmed it was all done amicably. Graves stepped down as the pioneering CEO and became the general manager and COO instead, while Kalanick ascended to the throne as the new Uber CEO[84]—he of the Scour and Red

https://techcrunch.com/2010/10/25/ubercab-now-just-uber-shares-cease-and-desist-orders/.
[84] Hartmans and McAlone, "Story."

Swoosh days, used to facing live fire and other types of adversities head-on. I guess, at this point, Kalanick was completely recovered from his burnout and no longer had any doubts that Uber was the next big thing in the technology universe. The resistance to their app was an indicator.[85] He was raring for a fight.

With Kalanick as the lead Uber driver, the pace of growth continued to pick up. You must know that he had been characterized often enough as a very aggressive salesman, so what ensued when he assumed company leadership was nothing short of masterful maneuvering into new markets. He was most likely able to do all that aided in a big way by the just concluded Series A funding.[86] At that time, the primary investor was Benchmark Capital, a VC firm known to enter companies like Dropbox, Twitter, and a few others at their early stages.[87]

The next destination on the Uber route was New York City in May 2011,[88] setting it against one of the strongest (in my opinion) omnipresent taxi medallion systems in the United States of

---

[85] Kalanick, "Startup."

[86] *Ibid.*

[87] *Wikipedia*, s.v. "Timeline of Uber," accessed March 11, 2019, https://en.wikipedia.org/wiki/Timeline_of_Uber.

[88] *Ibid.*

America (it was in Brooklyn in 2014 that I had my first-ever Uber and Airbnb experiences simultaneously, so New York will always be memorable to me in that way).

What surprised me about the city was the fact that people had already been trying to use Uber—well, at least to open the app anyway—even before it had made its services available there.[89] That data was available to see from slides that Kalanick presented at a launch party to celebrate the new market.[90] Clearly, Kalanick and Camp weren't the only people dissatisfied with the status quo in the taxi industry. There was definite momentum to Uber's rollout. People were showing impatience for it to register a blip on their radar.

Four months after their start in New York, Chicago went live on the Uber app in September 2011. Then came Boston, DC, Seattle, and more, one after the other. There was no stopping the US expansion. But let's face it: not everything was ideal in the US rollout. As I said, the San

---

[89] Erick Schonfeld, "Uber CEO on His 'Official' NYC Launch: 'Congestion Is a Bitch' (Video and Heatmaps)," TechCrunch, accessed March 11, 2019, https://techcrunch.com/2011/05/04/uber-screenshots-video/.
[90] *Ibid*.

Francisco resistance was just the beginning of a counter-Uber faction. Take for instance what happened in DC, according to Rachel Holt, who was tasked at that time to establish operations in the national capital.[91]

The first time Holt found out that DC had a problem with their service was through Twitter, not even a direct and official communication to their office. A posted tweet said that the taxi commissioner had declared the Uber setup illegal, without citing which rules had actually been broken. This happened less than a month after the official launch, in January 2012. Soon after the public announcement on the social media platform, the said commissioner requested for a ride and Holt cleared it, since she didn't feel like they had flouted any laws. The commissioner's destination was the Mayflower Hotel, where the press was waiting to witness what he did next (supposedly on a called-in tip from him or at least from his office—and you should know that the hotel is actually a favored venue for such DC spectacles). He had the Uber driver's vehicle impounded and slapped the poor guy with tickets worth about $2,000. After Holt scrambled the rest of the day to assure other

[91] Lashinsky, "Uber."

drivers that the company had their backs, Uber had more drivers on DC roads that evening than they ever had since December 2011.[92]

Anyway, all that antagonism was in the past and remained there. In spite of its rocky start at the nation's capital, Uber still managed to make inroads into the sacrosanct halls of Capitol Hill. In recent years, it had hired key personnel to petition for changes in federal policies affecting its industry and to position itself as an important lobby. At least one article acknowledged the company's evolution: "In just a few years, Uber has transformed from a scrappy startup to a Washington powerhouse—a path traveled by many tech companies but one that was largely unexpected for the nascent ride-hailing industry."[93] Without a doubt, Kalanick was earning his keep because that happened under his watch.

The year 2011 was capped by Uber's first expansion into an overseas market, which just had to be Paris, of course. It began in the same month as DC did. Coming back full circle to

---

[92] *Ibid*.
[93] Melanie Zanona and David McCabe, "Uber's Drive to Be a DC Powerhouse," *Hill*, January 25, 2017, https://thehill.com/policy/transportation/315960-ubers-drive-to-be-a-dc-powerhouse.

their point of convergence must have been deeply satisfying to the founders, especially with Kalanick given the floor at that year's LeWeb to talk about their plans for Europe. His bold announcement was that Uber was going to expand to two cities every month and have a total of about 25 cities in 13 to 14 months.[94] In context, it did not at all sound like an overly ambitious and unreachable plan because of consistent investor interest in the company. At this point, not even two years into its operations, Uber was proving it was a viable opportunity for investments and the proof was in the Series B funding that occurred just two days after the Paris inauguration.[95] Supposedly, one of the investors in this particular round happened to be Shawn Corey Carter aka Jay-Z, premier entertainer, entrepreneur, and record executive.[96]

Six months later, in July 2012, the company introduced a new type of ride, the UberX, which

---

[94] Stephen Shankland, "Car Service Uber Raises $32 Million, Launches in Paris," CNET, December 7, 2011, https://www.cnet.com/news/car-service-uber-raises-32-million-launches-in-paris/.

[95] *Wikipedia*, "Timeline."

[96] Leela Sanikop, "9 Investments That Will Help Make Jay-Z the First Billionaire in Hip-hop," Moguldom, June 2, 2017, https://moguldom.com/7240/9-investments-that-will-help-make-jay-z-the-first-billionaire-in-hip-hop/2/.

was unlike the UberBLACK (town-car rival in look and price) in that it was cheaper by about 35 percent and allowed the use of non-luxury vehicles.[97] That signaled the start of new products and services at Uber. Not only did Uber fine-tune so many aspects of their ride-hailing service (for example, adding more price options and using non-vehicle selections like boats and motorbikes, depending on the sociocultural context, no doubt), but they completely overhauled their company to be so much more than about ride-hailing. Because many of the said products and services were considered so unusual for Uber to undertake or simply unexpected, I will discuss just a few but most important of them separately in the next chapter covering innovations. But for now, let me continue with my narration about Uber's territorial growth. Before the year 2012 ended, in the month of November, Uber began plying the streets of Sydney, Australia.[98] G'day, mate!

With European and Australian developments happening at a consistent pace for the company, the next step towards international reach was appropriately enough into Mexico City in June

[97] *Wikipedia*, s.v. "Uber," accessed March 11, 2019, https://en.wikipedia.org/wiki/Uber.

[98] "History," Uber, accessed March 11, 2019, https://www.uber.com/en-KE/newsroom/history/.

2013, its first foray south of the US border and its first city in Latin America. Hopefully, that one was especially very sweet for Salazar. Although he has barely appeared in this narrative since I mentioned his meeting with Camp in 2008, he is sometimes considered, arguably, the founding architect of the actual technology on which Uber runs,[99] the third part of the cofounding trinity. Hence, an introduction of Salazar's blood-sweat-and-tears into his birthplace somehow seemed apropos, a full-circle return. Much like Paris must have been to Kalanick and Camp.

In quick succession after the Mexico City launch, Uber entered the Asian market via Taipei in July 2013 and Africa starting with Johannesburg in South Africa a month later. In the same month of the African opening, Uber received yet another infusion of funding from its Series C. This time around, one of its most prominent investors was Google Ventures[100] or GV, as it is known now. It is the venture capital investment arm of Alphabet Inc.,[101] which in

[99] "Oscar Salazar," SEO, accessed March 16, 2019, https://www.seo-usa.org/about/board-of-directors/oscar-salazar/.
[100] *Wikipedia*, "Timeline."
[101] *Wikipedia*, s.v. "GV (Company)," accessed March 11, 2019, https://en.wikipedia.org/wiki/GV_(company).

turn is the parent company of all things Google, including everything that used to be merely Google subsidiaries.

Because of sheer population density, two important international markets that Uber entered were India (with Bangalore as its first port of call, in August 2013)[102] and, of course, China via Shanghai in February 2014.[103] Sixteen months after the official launch, a peek into its India-based operations showed that it had the largest network of metropolitan areas (11 cities, until Uber China overtook it and before said Uber China lost the territory to a stronger, homegrown operator) outside the United States of America, growing by almost one city per month.

For a foreign brand, its progress was quite remarkable in the extremely unpredictable temperament of the country. And as with some of its previous market entries, Uber also had a faceoff with Indian politicians and regulators. However, sadly, the biggest controversy that came out of the subcontinent in those early days

---

[102] *Wikipedia*, "Timeline."

[103] Liu Jiayi, "Uber Officially Enters China with Shanghai Launch," ZDNet, February 14, 2014, https://www.zdnet.com/article/uber-officially-enters-china-with-shanghai-launch/.

wasn't even about regulation issues. What hit the international wires was the news of a male Uber driver raping his female passenger in the outskirts of Delhi. Many sectors of society cried for Uber's shutdown after that, which the government did until compliance standards were met.[104] Two important outcomes from the India rape incident was the introduction of a panic button and a tracking feature right on the app itself.[105]

That particular scandal should have just been laid to rest, except that three years later, in December 2017, it was reported that the Indian rape victim (now a resident of Texas) had just settled out of court with Uber (again, as she had also named the company in the first criminal case versus the rapist) in her defamation lawsuit filed against it.[106] Apparently, senior staff at

---

[104] Eric Bellman and Dhanya Ann Thoppil, "How Did Uber Go from Nowhere to Everywhere in India?" *Wall Street Journal*, December 10, 2014, https://blogs.wsj.com/indiarealtime/2014/12/10/how-did-uber-go-from-nowhere-to-everywhere-in-india/.
[105] Saritha Rai, "Uber Gets Serious about Passenger Safety in India, Introduces Panic Button," *Forbes*, February 12, 2015, https://www.forbes.com/sites/saritharai/2015/02/12/uber-gets-serious-about-passenger-safety-in-india-introduces-panic-button/#174118aa3cf8.
[106] "Uber Settles Defamation Lawsuit Filed by Indian Rape Victim," BBC, December 9, 2017, https://www.bbc.com/news/world-us-canada-42291495.

Uber, including Kalanick himself, had doubted her story and surmised that she had made it up to destroy their business in collusion with a rival company. Someone at Uber even had the victim's medical records obtained in the hope of digging up dirt to prove her claim false. The settlement was done in San Francisco, right where HQ stood.

Uber's story in China was very different. It worked with a local car rental company to recruit drivers instead of opening its applications to all interested individuals out there, as it did in the United States and most other territories.[107] It soon went beyond Shanghai into other key cities like Beijing, Guangzhou, Shenzhen, and many more. It seemed to have created an impressively wide network of operations, but "it never felt like they were established enough in China. People kept saying: 'The Chinese government will never favor foreign competition in the market and will shut them down.'"[108] Interestingly enough, when Uber's downfall in China did happen, it

---

[107] Jiayi, "Uber."

[108] Shlomo Freund, "A Short History of Uber in China: Was It a Failure?" *Forbes*, August 15, 2016, https://www.forbes.com/sites/shlomofreund/2016/08/15/a-short-history-of-uber-in-china-was-it-a-failure/#630e8a673386.

wasn't really the government to blame—at least, not directly. It simply got outmaneuvered by a very tough local competition in the form of Didi Kuaidi, which came into existence in February 2015 with the merger of two Uber rivals, Didi Dache, and Kuaidi Dache.[109] Their combined forces made them a larger company than Uber.[110]

Even when Uber received a $1.2 billion investment from Baidu, China's equivalent to Google, it still was not enough to go up against the $4 billion combined treasure chest Didi Kuaidi (which later became known as Didi Chuxing[111]) received from the likes of China Investment Corporation, Capital International Private Equity Funds, Ping An Ventures, and Apple.[112] Fast forward then to 2016, when Uber finally threw in the towel and was acquired by the Chinese company, raising the latter's valuation to $35 billion: Didi Chuxing's $28 billion valuations plus Uber China's $7 billion valuations. With the merger and acquisition, Uber became a minority shareholder of the

---

[109] Freund, "History."
[110] *Wikipedia*, "Timeline."
[111] *Wikipedia*, s.v. "DiDi," accessed March 11, 2019, https://en.wikipedia.org/wiki/DiDi.
[112] Freund, "History."

Chinese company at 5.89 percent.[113]

Painful as the China expedition was (Uber burned through $2 billion in two years, trying to chip away at its competitors' market share[114]), overall, Uber continued to grow from strength to strength. Back to the other populous Uber market, in India, it received an undisclosed amount of investment from Tata Opportunities, a private equity fund based in Mumbai,[115] in August 2015. Although the figure was not publicized, an anonymous source said that it may have been between $75 to 100 million.[116] At Uber HQ, several more investment rounds happened. As of this writing, it has had 22 cycles already, totaling $24.2 billion in funds

---

[113] Arjun Kharpal, "Taxi App Rival Didi Chuxing to Buy Uber's China Business in $35 Billion Deal," CNBC, August 1, 2016, https://www.cnbc.com/2016/08/01/chinas-didi-chuxing-to-acquire-ubers-chinese-operations-wsj.html.

[114] ---, "5 Reasons Why Uber Sold Its China Business to Didi Chuxing," CNBC, August 1, 2016, https://www.cnbc.com/2016/08/01/5-reasons-why-uber-sold-its-china-business-to-didi-chuxing.html.

[115] "About," Tata Opportunities Fund, accessed March 11, 2019, https://www.tataopportunitiesfund.com/about-us.html.

[116] Pooja Sarkar and Ashna Ambre, "Uber Raises up to $100 Million from Tata Fund," Live Mint, August 20, 2015, https://www.livemint.com/Companies/3stUSqNMHesUdVi8NmLXTK/Uber-gets-investment-from-Tata-Capital-Fund-to-expand-in-Ind.html.

raised.[117]

There were also a few other casualties besides Uber China, although not as large in scale. It had to retreat from Austin, Texas, after an ordinance requiring its drivers to undergo fingerprint checks passed. It affected even its rival, Lyft, which also left the Texas metropolis in May 2016.[118] At that time, both companies felt that the background checks they did were already sufficient to weed out anyone with a record that could compromise the integrity of their organization. The additional requirements of fingerprints and other data reports served only to slow down their hiring processes, both claimed.[119] A good twist to the story was that, exactly a year later, they both returned to Austin after the Texas governor signed a law that transferred ride-hailing regulations from local governments to the state government.[120]

---

[117] "Uber Funding Rounds," Crunchbase, accessed March 11, 2019, https://www.crunchbase.com/organization/uber/funding_rounds/funding_rounds_list.

[118] *Wikipedia*, "Timeline."

[119] Charlie Osborne, "Uber, Lyft Return to Austin as Driver Fingerprint Rule Overturned," ZDNet, May 30, 2017, https://www.zdnet.com/article/uber-lyft-return-to-austin-as-texas-fingerprint-rule-dismissed/.

[120] *Ibid*.

In July 2016, Uber departed from Budapest, Hungary, because of prohibitive government legislation, not to mention months-long protests by local taxi drivers.[121] The law determined internet access and how "illegal dispatch services" could be blocked from it.[122] Obviously, Uber was counted among those illegals. According to the general manager of Uber in central Europe, the law was akin to a forced suspension, affecting both users and drivers alike. It left the company with no choice but to pull out. To date, there are no signs of a possible return any time soon or in the far future.

In the Philippines, Uber shut down in April 2018 as part of its plan for regional integration with Grab, Uber's Singapore-based rival, which already had a firm and ever-broadening footprint in Southeast Asia.[123] Of course, the merger wasn't just about niceties and

---

[121] Krisztina Than and Krisztina Fenyo, "Uber to Suspend Operations in Hungary Due to Government Legislation," Reuters, July 13, 2016, https://www.reuters.com/article/us-uber-hungary-exit/uber-to-suspend-operations-in-hungary-due-to-govt-legislation-idUSKCN0ZT0RS.

[122] *Ibid*.

[123] Cliff Venzon, "Uber to End Service in the Philippines on Monday," *Nikkei Asian Review*, April 16, 2018, https://asia.nikkei.com/Business/Companies/Uber-Grab-moves-closer-to-Southeast-Asian-integration.

bonhomie. In truth, Uber appeared to be losing money in the ASEAN territories.[124] By selling its SEA business to Grab, it was also securing an overall stake in the firm, a 27.5 percent stake to be exact.[125] The deal drew the attention of regulators not only in the Philippines but also in Malaysia, Vietnam, and Singapore. Everybody was concerned about the resulting monopoly and how it could affect prices, quality of service, driver compensation, and the like. In the end, Singapore and the Philippines fined both companies after their respective investigations. Singapore slapped Grab and Uber $9.5 million, and the Philippines charged them $296,873 for their failure to abide by rules ensuring fairness to consumers and the haste by which they consummated the transaction.[126]

---

[124] Neil Jerome Morales, "Philippines Sets Rules for 'Virtual Monopolist' Grab after Uber Deal," Reuters, August 10, 2018, https://www.reuters.com/article/us-uber-grab-philippines/philippines-sets-rules-for-virtual-monopolist-grab-after-uber-deal-idUSKBN1KV0VI.

[125] Abhimanyu Ghoshal, "Uber's Southeast Asia Operations Acquired by Grab," Next Web, accessed March 11, 2019, https://thenextweb.com/asia/2018/03/26/ubers-southeast-asia-operations-acquired-by-grab/.

[126] Neil Jerome Morales, "Philippine Watchdog Fine Grab, Uber for Rushed Merger, Drop in Service Quality," Reuters, October 17, 2018, https://www.reuters.com/article/us-uber-grab-philippines/philippine-watchdog-fines-grab-uber-for-rushed-merger-drop-in-service-quality-idUSKCN1MR146.

In between the ebb and flow of Uber across the globe, innovations to its products and services popped up as milestones alongside geographical expansions on its timeline. Already, I had mentioned UberX, but even that was not really groundbreaking compared to the new menu of logistical goodies Uber created over the next few years. UberX was just an improvement to the car-riding experience, but Uber had its eyes set on more than just common land transportation. In a very literal way, the sky became the limit for the Uber geniuses over at San Francisco.

In the next chapter, I'll direct your attention to four trailblazing Uber innovations and all the good and bad they brought the company. I'll also introduce you to some of Uber's products and services contextualized to fit the cultures of their specific markets.

Chapter 4: That Uncommon Route from Point A to Point B

By definition, a transportation network company or TNC is an organization that connects drivers and passengers via a mobile phone app.[127] It is really supposed to be a rather simple equation with just three elements involved: passenger plus driver equals paid ride. However, in the case of Uber, it is fascinating and quite a conundrum whether or not to apply the label to it because it has become so much more than just about people and rides. I mean, for crying out loud, it now connects you to food, your healthcare clinic, and kittens.[128]

When Uber does something as radical as those examples, so many people very quickly attach the word "disruptive" to describe the impact its actions have on certain industries and sectors of society. Of course, most of the time that term is really meant to be a compliment, backhanded or not, to Uber. However, I also refer back to a

---

[127] *Wikipedia*, s.v. "Transportation Network Company," accessed March 11, 2019, https://en.wikipedia.org/wiki/Transportation_network_company.

[128] Uber, "History."

Camp interview[129] and reflect on something he said about the word.

While Camp was aware that it was meant to be flattering, he himself seemed uncomfortable about including it to descriptions of the kinds of things he, Kalanick, and their company did. They were merely trying to solve problems, to improve upon the status quo, to create something they wanted for themselves. They were not there deliberately to throw everybody off balance. And I think that's why the Uber team has had more hits than misses in its many innovations. Because they're not doing what they do for the shock value of it. They invent with themselves as the first users.

Now in surveying Uber's most innovative products and services, I can clearly see its motives. It is really all about conveniences and efficiencies, not disruption per se. To understand what I mean, take a look at some of its inventions and the serious money they have generated. At the same time, don't steer clear of the controversies surrounding them. I mention them here because they're part of Uber's history for good or ill, putting everything in a proper, balanced perspective.

---

[129] Camp, "Mentality."

Uber Eats

Back in 2014, while Uber was entering China and spreading throughout its many metropolitan areas for the first time, it also created a new platform, UberFRESH, which debuted in Santa Monica, California.[130] Just like Uber itself, UberFRESH was meant to create an easier way for doing a commonplace activity, online food ordering and delivery.

In order to make it work, Uber recruited restaurants to sign up as partners, whose menus, (full or partial, depending on the restaurant) became available and viewable on the Uber site. From there, it was possible for anyone to order food from the allied establishments and have it delivered to the hungry customer's precise location at a reasonable fee paid for by the latter. This was a huge opportunity for both restaurants and customers. For the restaurants, especially those that did not have the resources or infrastructure to receive orders online and/or to do deliveries, it provided them a new revenue stream by simply piggybacking on the established logistics of Uber. Deliveries could be done by means of cars, bikes, or motorbikes, or on foot. For the

---

[130] *Wikipedia*, s.v. "Uber Eats," accessed March 11, 2019, https://en.wikipedia.org/wiki/Uber_Eats.

customers, it opened up the possibility of satisfying their wildest foodie cravings, even if the object of their desire was 100 miles away, across a state line (of course, I'm just trying to be funny here. The delivery distance is still dependent on what Uber and the restaurant itself considered best without sacrificing safety and food quality.). I'm pretty sure hapless husbands with pregnant wives now have Uber Eats as their first stop for appeasing their hangry spouses.

Clearly, UberFRESH (renamed UberEATS a year later and then eventually just Uber Eats, without the stylized syntax) is a money-making winner. In 2018, estimates show that it delivered more than $6 billion worth of food across the globe.[131] From that number, Uber received 30 percent for its services plus the delivery fee paid by the customer. From that total, it deducted what was contractually due to the driver, leaving it with still a lot of money for the piggy bank. In this year, 2019, that could

---

[131] Biz Carson, "Uber's Secret Gold Mine: How Uber Eats Is Turning into a Billion-Dollar Business to Rival Grubhub," *Forbes*, February 6, 2019, https://www.forbes.com/sites/bizcarson/2019/02/06/ubers-secret-gold-mine-how-uber-eats-is-turning-into-a-billion-dollar-business-to-rival-grubhub/#6098e4421fa9.

mean at least $1 billion.[132] With an IPO still in the works, as of this writing, Uber Eats could likely be an attractive added factor to the overall valuation of the company. Until the IPO actually happens, it's anybody's guess how Uber will be able to justify its sky-high price tag. I can readily tell you that the annual revenues of Uber Eats will be a definite contributor to that.

Since 2015, at the same time it renamed itself, Uber Eats has had its own spin-off app, separate and different from the original Uber app. That meant only one thing: increased expediency literally at the customer's fingertips. And when it comes to humans and their food, you don't really want to keep them waiting too long. The fact that Uber Eats is now one of the largest food-delivery services on Earth should show you that people want their food. And fast.[133] And they will pay a premium without raising an eyebrow (most of the time) for as long as it is taken, with a smile and other customer courtesies, right to their doorstep, not sent sailing up to the roof a la *Breaking Bad*.

In recent times, there's been a bit of confusion

---

[132] Carson, "Secret."

[133] *Ibid*.

concerning their new pricing scheme,[134] but overall, Uber Eats is keeping pace with DoorDash and Grubhub, its main competitors. What is telling is that Grubhub is losing value as a company and a market leader ($7 billion stock market value, baby!) because of the stiff competition that the two others are giving it.[135] That bodes well for Uber Eats, of course, because it can gain more traction in introducing new aspects to its delivery service.

Already, there was a report from Down Under that a supermarket was tying up with Uber Eats to deliver its ready-made, ready-to-heat, and grab-and-go meals to your home, office, or wherever you happened to be.[136] Nope, Uber wasn't going to do grocery deliveries, just ready-

[134] Shannon Liao, "Uber Eats Rolls Out Confusing New Fees— Here's What They Mean," Verge, March 19, 2019, https://www.theverge.com/2019/3/19/18272791/uber-eats-new-booking-delivery-service-fees-confusion-meaning.
[135] Lauren Feiner, "Grubhub Sinks as Analysts Say It's Struggling to Keep Pace with Uber Eats and DoorDash," CNBC, March 19, 2019, https://www.cnbc.com/2019/03/19/grubhub-sinks-as-it-loses-share-to-ubereats-and-doordash.html.
[136] Natassia Chrysanthos, "Coles Quietly Expands Uber Eats Trial to Deliver Supermarket Essentials," *Sydney Morning Herald*, March 21, 2019, https://www.smh.com.au/business/companies/coles-quietly-expands-ubereats-trial-to-deliver-supermarket-essentials-20190319-p515k9.html.

to-eat food for your mouth to feast on. Experts were placing a bet on its success simply because, to so many people, time is even more valuable than money. The (premium) delivery fee would seem negligible compared to what could and would be lost if you trekked to a restaurant or convenience store yourself. Even a Woolworths boss expressed more worry about the rise of Uber Eats than of Amazon because of the high level of convenience it offered its users.[137] Very soon, you and I can expect that Uber Eats will have the same global coverage as Uber or wider. It's simply a sign of the times. Convenience is king.

Advanced Technologies Group

If you just took its name at face value, you would think Advanced Technologies Group was an arm of NASA or some other space agency. You might then be disappointed to discover that this is the official name of that branch in the Uber business organization, which has to do with

---

[137] Patrick Hatch, "Why Woolies Boss Thinks Uber Eats Is a Bigger Threat Than Amazon," *Sunday Morning Herald*, February 24, 2018, https://www.smh.com.au/business/companies/why-woolies-boss-thinks-uber-eats-is-a-bigger-threat-than-amazon-20180223-p4z1gp.html.

self-driving cars.

You must've been living under a rock or in Atlantis not to know about this development in transportation. It is no longer just part of a sci-fi movie but reality to have driverless vehicles on the road. Thanks to a lot of science and technology, the future of transportation is now right here. Much of what is currently being done in ATG is still in the experimental stage though. On its webpage, it says, "If successful, these vehicles make our roads safer and transportation more affordable for everyone."[138] IF. And I'll tell you why it's still an "if" in a few. But first, let me give you a bit of background about ATG.

Uber's start in this particular research-and-development initiative was quite a rocky event, considering that it had siphoned off about 50 employees from the robotics center of Carnegie Mellon University, starting in January 2015 all the way up to May of the same year. I'm not even talking about just the rank and file but also the top administrators in the lab.[139] Most, if not all,

---

[138] "The Future of Transportation," Uber, accessed March 11, 2019, https://www.uber.com/info/atg/.

[139] Josh Lowensohn, "Uber Gutted Carnegie Mellon's Top Robotics Lab to Build Self-driving Cars," Verge, May 19, 2015,

of them were involved in vehicle autonomy. When they moved down the road to their new workplace, they carried with them the one most important asset that was especially worth poaching: the stuff inside their brains, the intellectual properties that mattered. Shortly after the poaching began in January, the university and Uber representatives came out to say that it was a strategic partnership for both of them, but insiders had a different story to tell and spoke of the confusion that ensued with the personnel departures.[140]

The appropriation of CMU human resources was just the beginning of ATG controversies. In December 2016, Uber attempted to do a pilot for its self-driving vehicles in California, but regulators shut it down because it didn't even have any permits. To top it off, the autonomous vehicles were actually quite the road hazard by running red lights once in a while. Cyclists also raised concerns about their safety, if even one vehicle accidentally strayed into their lane.[141]

---

https://www.theverge.com/transportation/2015/5/19/8622831/uber-self-driving-cars-carnegie-mellon-poached.
[140] *Ibid.*
[141] Sam Levin, "Uber's Scandals, Blunders, and PR Disasters: The Full List," *Guardian*, June 28, 2017, https://www.theguardian.com/technology/2017/jun/18/uber-travis-kalanick-scandal-pr-disaster-timeline.

Two months later, in February 2017, Waymo, Alphabet's previous self-driving car division filed a lawsuit against Uber for stealing its technology to skip steps in its R & D and get ahead of everybody else. Supposedly, the dastardly deed was accomplished when the latter bought Otto, a startup established by a former Google engineer. In turn, that engineer had thousands of Google files in his possession, which included the trade secrets that prompted the Waymo case.[142] Does theft to get ahead of research sound familiar? Yeah, I thought so, too. After a year of battling it out in court, a settlement was reached in February 2018, giving Waymo a .34 percent stake in Uber worth $245 million.[143] It came with conditions that Uber couldn't use any secret sauce from the IP haul it secured via Otto.

And then there was the blunder that cost somebody her life. In March 2018, Elaine Herzberg was killed while jaywalking across a road, when one of Uber's self-driving vehicles failed to do an emergency stop. As it turned out,

---

[142] Anita Balakrishnan, Jillian D'Onfro, Deirdre Bosa, and Paayal Zaveri, "Uber Settles Dispute with Alphabet's Self-driving Car Unit," CNBC, February 9, 2018, https://www.cnbc.com/2018/02/09/uber-waymo-lawsuit-settlement.html.
[143] *Ibid.*

the very system that could have saved Herzberg's life was actually turned off at the time of the crash to provide a smoother riding experience for the passenger on board. So even if the car had sensed her presence in its immediate vicinity, the disabled braking system wouldn't have been able to kick in.[144]

Uber was very quick to settle with the victim's family for an undisclosed amount within a few weeks of the accident. It also suspended its operations following the tragedy.[145] At least, on public roads for the next nine months following the incident. Thereafter, Uber resumed its tests but only in a small section of a Pittsburgh neighborhood. All companies that had self-driving experiments going on, not just Uber, definitely recalibrated their operations to avoid a similar accident in the future.[146]

---

[144] Meriame Berboucha, "Uber Self-Driving Car Crash: What Really Happened?" *Forbes*, May 28, 2018, https://www.forbes.com/sites/meriameberboucha/2018/05/28/uber-self-driving-car-crash-what-really-happened/#3a6cf67c4dc4.

[145] Reuters, "Uber Settles with Family of Woman Killed by Self-Driving Car," *Guardian*, March 29, 2019, https://www.theguardian.com/technology/2018/mar/29/uber-settles-with-family-of-woman-killed-by-self-driving-car.

[146] Aarian Marshall, "1 Year after Uber's Fatal Crash, Robocars Carry On Quietly," Wired, March 18, 2019,

One year after the incident, the victim's daughter filed a civil case against the state of Arizona and the city of Tempe for creating conditions that made roads unsafe for people like her mother.[147] How that case will affect the future of ATG is anyone's guess, which is why higher safety standards courtesy of self-driving vehicles remains a big IF.

Uber Elevate

An Uber innovation that is still very much in the conceptual stage but well worth mentioning here anyway is Elevate, which is essentially Uber for the skies. The company is working on developing a fleet of four-person aircrafts capable of doing vertical landings and takeoffs. Electric Vertical-Takeoff-and-Landing (eVTOL) taxis are supposed to be ride-shares in urban markets. Once realized, they are meant to provide three hours of flight time at 150 mph.[148]

---

https://www.wired.com/story/uber-crash-elaine-herzberg-anniversary-safety-self-driving/.

[147] Ryan Randazzo, "Family of Woman Killed in Crash with Self-Driving Uber Sues Arizona, Tempe," *AZ Central*, March 19, 2019,
https://www.azcentral.com/story/news/local/tempe/2019/03/19/arizona-city-tempe-sued-family-uber-self-driving-car-crash-victim-elaine-herzberg/3207598002/.

[148] Nicolas Zart, "Uber Elevate: Future of Air Taxis = 3 Hours of Flight, 150 MPH, 4 Passengers," Clean Technica, February

Think of what that convenience could mean for you. No more random wait times in city traffic!

Because such a service requires specific infrastructure in place, Uber does not intend to roll it out as widely as it had done for its original ride-hailing operations. So far, it has narrowed down its list to Dallas and Los Angeles as the first two inaugural cities. Five countries are also in the running for a third launch location: Japan, France, Brazil, Australia, and India. With its foray into airspace and drones becoming more ubiquitous than ever before, discussions on airborne Uber Eats are not too far behind.[149]

Uber Works

There seems to be no stopping the cooks at Uber who have come up with a new idea in their kitchen. In late 2018, Uber started a new logistical business called Uber Works, which provides on-demand staffing. Still very much in

---

15, 2019, https://cleantechnica.com/2019/02/15/uber-elevate-future-of-air-taxis-3-hours-of-flight-150-mph-4-passengers/.

[149] Andrew J. Hawkins, "Uber Narrows Its Search for International City to Host 'Flying Taxis,'" Verge, August 30, 2018,
https://www.theverge.com/2018/8/30/17795588/uber-elevate-flying-car-international-city-search-drone.

its infancy, Uber Works is one of the company's moves towards diversification as it prepares for an IPO. It is also expected to be a new revenue stream for Uber.[150]

As a service, Uber Works is meant to ease the pain of businesses in need of short-term workers like waiters or security guards during their special events and corporate functions.[151] It had already trialed in Los Angeles. Although its pilot does not include Uber's current network of drivers, it may be viewed as potential additional income for them.[152]

This particular initiative falls under the jurisdiction of Rachel Holt.[153] Remember her from the DC incident I told you about in the previous chapter? Well, it is now Holt's responsibility to ensure that new projects like this and other "mobility services like bikes, scooters, car rentals, and public transit integration"[154] are seamlessly brought into Uber operations. You can imagine how essential her

---

[150] O'Kane, "Uber."

[151] Ibid.

[152] Megan Rose Dickey, "Uber Is Developing an On-demand Staffing Business," TechCrunch, accessed March 11, 2019, https://techcrunch.com/2018/10/18/uber-is-developing-an-on-demand-staffing-business/.

[153] Dickey, "Uber."

[154] Ibid.

job is especially in light of the looming IPO. Whether or not Uber Works will rake in money has yet to be determined. It's way too early to tell. One thing is clear though, it will be an important factor to consider as potential investors move in to determine the true valuation of the company.

Country-Specific Uber Services

Speaking of mobility services, if you haven't ever stepped out of your urban setting where only UberX registers as your ride type, then you're missing out on quite a number of other options in the menu of Uber products and services. Of course, most of these rides are very specific to the cultural context of the company's markets, so you truly won't get to experience them, unless you hop on a plane and fly across the world to try them out. It's always a good move on the part of a company, when it responds to and respects the local population's deeply entrenched habits and choices.

Take for instance UberAUTO, which is an auto rickshaw service available only in India, Sri Lanka, and Pakistan.[155] It is a motorized improvement on the classic rickshaw, which

---

[155] *Wikipedia*, "Uber."

used to be powered either by pulling or pedaling (on a bike). The equivalent of that in Kenya would be the Boda, which is essentially a motorbike for hire, with you riding behind the driver as the paying passenger. *Bodaboda* is the Swahili term for a motorcycle. The East African country also has Chapchap,[156] which are lower-end Uber cars much smaller than the standard fare the company allows. Because of their size and maneuverability, they are great for getting through the congestion of Nairobi traffic. Similar to Uber's adaptation of the word *bodaboda*, *chapchap* is a Sheng (mixed Swahili-English slang) term for "quickly," which makes it appropriate for this kind of ride.

UberBOAT is a speedboat employed as a water taxi in places like the Croatian coast in summer. It was also demonstrated in Miami Art Week, as a means of transportation across Biscayne Bay. Bosporus Strait in Istanbul has also been a site (during the summer) of this type of Uber ride.[157]

Aside from these location-specific rides, Uber has also shown responsiveness to other sociocultural realities like elderly assistance and physical disabilities (UberASSIST, UberWAV, and UberHEALTH). It knows how to treat its

---

[156] *Ibid.*
[157] *Ibid.*

users' loved ones very well (UberKIDS and UberPETS). It knows that riding solo isn't always fun or economical (UberPOOL). And it's certainly aware that its users sometimes want to drive the vehicle themselves (UberBike and Uber Rent). UberESPAÑOL is even there for users who want Spanish-speaking drivers to give them a ride.[158]

In all, when you survey their menu further, you can see that Uber really tries to be that logistics company that preempts your needs.

However, as with all humongous companies, it simply cannot escape the reality that scandals and controversies can happen to the very best of them. Uber has certainly had its fair share. I've already mentioned a few in this chapter and previous ones, but we have yet to discuss the zingers, some of which brought about the downfall—sadly or not, depending on your loyalties—of Kalanick himself.

---

[158] *Wikipedia*, "Uber."

Chapter 5: Even Superhighways Have Cracks, Potholes, and Assholes

Sadly, you can't get to be as big as Uber without suffering from lapses due to hubris. It is the nature of the beast. When you climb up to unimaginable peaks as one of the highest-valued tech companies across the globe, it is easy to lose your bearings because you can't see the ground anymore underneath your feet. All that you feel is the wind on your face and the immense freedom that comes from being able to spread your wings in all that wide open space on your very own (metaphorical) Everest. Because no one else is standing beside you to get in your way.

Since its creation in 2009, Uber has dealt with all the drama and glory associated with growing a business. Some of its early issues stemmed from the drivers themselves and the drivers' relationship with the company. Those were likely expected because they are akin to employer-employee squabbles (although Uber has always maintained and will very likely continue to maintain that their drivers are not their employees per se).

However, in recent years, Uber has had to deal with more than just those kinds of issues. Many controversies have emerged concerning its business practices and the underhanded ways it deals with its competitors. It has even become a statistic in stories of privacy breaches brought about by its own doing.

One of Uber's biggest scandals though focuses on its innate corporate culture, which so many people have attributed to Kalanick's own misogynistic, sexist behavior. His attitude and words had somehow seeped through to the rest of management and down to the rank and file. It had given almost everybody else in Uber the permission to act badly. And that signaled the beginning of Kalanick's end.

Uber Drivers Driving Uber Up a Wall

When Uber was still new and trying to establish its own brand, very few people outside the company fully understood just how it worked. The consumer-facing mobile phone app didn't tell anybody anything about how drivers were related to Uber itself. That was part of the back office. I think even the drivers themselves needed that relationship to be defined properly, which led to a class-action lawsuit against the company.

That litigation started way back in December 2013.[159] On behalf of 350,000 former and current Uber drivers in both Massachusetts and California, Attorney Shannon Liss-Riordan filed the first documents against the company.[160] The drivers contended that they should be treated like employees by Uber. This meant they must be entitled to reimbursements for their vehicle maintenance and gas expenses.[161] In addition, it should also allow them to receive benefits (healthcare, for instance) and a minimum wage. However, Uber did not budge from its position: drivers were not their employees but independent contractors. What Uber was contracted to provide them was access to the driver-facing app and just that to connect them to their

---

[159] Kate Taylor, "40 of the Biggest Scandals in Uber History," Business Insider, November 24, 2017, https://www.businessinsider.com/uber-company-scandals-and-controversies-2017-11?IR=T.

[160] Madison Malone Kircher, "How Uber Got Here," *New York Magazine*, March 8, 2017, http://nymag.com/intelligencer/article/dramatic-history-ride-hailing-app-uber-and-ceo-kalanick.html.

[161] Dan Levine, "Uber Drivers Granted Class Action Status in Lawsuit over Employment," Reuters, September 1, 2015, https://www.reuters.com/article/us-uber-tech-drivers-lawsuit-idUSKCN0R14O920150901.

potential passengers. Uber was merely a conduit for drivers to conduct their own business.

The lawsuit didn't receive any sort of ruling until early 2015, when the presiding judge declared that the Uber case could go into a jury trial. The same decision was reached by another judge, who was handling a separate but similar case filed by Lyft drivers against, well, Lyft, of course.[162] Many parties from various sectors of the society were watching both the proceedings very closely because of the ramifications they would have on the business models of ride-hailing companies, the setups of the gig, on-demand, and sharing economies, and the valuations of Uber and Lyft. The judge in the Lyft case said something rather curious when he said that the drivers didn't appear to be either employees or independent contractors, in the strictest sense of both terms. He acknowledged the apparent limitations of his office and the jury's by saying that they were being given 20th-century definitions for 21st-century issues.[163] There were no precedents to follow, which made

---

[162] Ellen Huet, "Juries to Decide Landmark Cases against Uber and Lyft," *Forbes*, March 11, 2015, https://www.forbes.com/sites/ellenhuet/2015/03/11/lyft-uber-employee-jury-trial-ruling/#65707b3964b9.
[163] *Ibid*.

the result of their case a landmark to guide future litigation.

Later that same year, in late August, a US district judge gave class-action status to the Liss-Riordan filing, which gave a stronger clout to the drivers on how their compensation or settlement should look like.[164] It also made their position more attractive to draw additional drivers to their side. In April 2016, Uber agreed to settle the suit with a payout of $100 million to about, at that point, 385,000 drivers.[165]

The settlement allowed Uber to continue treating its drivers as independent contractors, which definitely was welcome news even to its rivals with the same business model as theirs. It meant that none of the companies that overlapped with the gig economy one had to do a major overhaul of their operations because there was no real change to the status quo vis-à-vis company-driver relations. The court resolution also directed Uber to make an outright payment of $84 million to the drivers, with an additional $16 million to be paid to the

---

[164] Levine, "Uber."

[165] Arjun Kharpal, "Uber Settles for $100 Million in Lawsuit over Driver Status," CNBC, April 22, 2016, https://www.cnbc.com/2016/04/22/uber-makes-100-million-settlement-in-lawsuit-over-driver-status.html.

latter again should Uber become a publicly traded company.

However, that settlement never happened. For one, the drivers themselves felt it was not the best outcome for them. Douglas O'Connor, one of the three original filers of the lawsuit, said that many of their issues were not really addressed in the settlement. Foremost among the drivers' objections was how the amount of $100 million was computed. It did not seem sufficient to cover all the expenses they deemed the responsibility of Uber.[166] For sure, a number of them lashed out at Liss-Riordan.[167] If any of them felt that she had sold them out, I couldn't blame them. I might have felt the same way in their shoes, but Liss-Riordan maintained that it was best to accept the agreement or risk not receiving anything at all.[168]

Needless to say, a month after the planned

---

[166] Davey Alba, "Some Drivers Really Aren't Happy about the $100 Million Uber Settlement," Wired, May 16, 2016, https://www.wired.com/2016/05/drivers-really-arent-happy-100m-uber-settlement/.

[167] Johana Bhuiyan, "Why the Uber Drivers' Lawyer Settled Their Fight to Become Employees," Recode, April 30, 2016, https://www.recode.net/2016/4/30/11586570/uber-drivers-employees-contractors-lawyer.

[168] ---, "Judge Rejects Uber's $100 Million Settlement with Drivers," Wired, August 8, 2016, https://www.wired.com/2016/08/uber-settlement-rejected/.

settlement was announced, O'Connor came back into the public eye, with a new filing to counter the settlement and new representation to continue the fight for what he felt were his and his fellow drivers' rights. Regardless of the drivers' sentiments, however, there was a bigger reason why the settlement wasn't fulfilled. In August 2016, a federal judge rejected it, calling it unfair, inadequate, and unreasonable.[169] And so the case carried on.

In September 2018, a major victory went to Uber, when the Ninth US Circuit Court of Appeals reversed the class certification order. This meant that thousands of drivers previously included in the class-action lawsuit could no longer be counted in it because they were covered under an arbitration clause.[170] The appeals court ruled that their contracts were valid and enforceable.[171] If they wanted their

---

[169] *Ibid*.

[170] Andrew J. Hawkins, "Uber Scores a Big Win in Legal Fight to Keep Drivers as Independent Contractors," Verge, September 25, 2018, https://www.theverge.com/2018/9/25/17901284/uber-drivers-independent-contractors-vs-employees-legal-fight.

[171] Megan Rose Dickey, "Uber Agrees to Pay Drivers $20 Million to Settle Independent Contractor," TechCrunch, March 12, 2019, https://techcrunch.com/2019/03/12/uber-agrees-to-pay-drivers-20-million-to-settle-independent-contractor-lawsuit/.

status as independent contractors to be converted to employees, they had to seek it as individuals.

Five months after that ruling was made, in March 2019, Uber agreed to pay $20 million to its drivers and keep them classified as independent contractors. Less money for a smaller number of drivers. And that was how the O'Connor case ended. Just in time, too, as Uber draws closer to an IPO.[172] That was a legal battle that clearly needed to be concluded to calm investors down.

Besides the O'Connor lawsuit between Uber and its drivers, there have also been those many other scandals and controversies involving individual drivers, which reflected badly on the company whether they liked it or not. I've already told you about the Indian driver who raped his passenger back in 2014. But even before that, other incidents had occurred that definitely did nothing to enhance Uber's image to the public.

---

[172] Therese Poletti, "Opinion: Uber Clears What Looked to Be an IPO Roadblock with $20 Million Settlement," MarketWatch, March 17, 2019, https://www.marketwatch.com/story/uber-clears-what-looked-to-be-an-ipo-roadblock-with-20-million-settlement-2019-03-12.

In September 2013, a passenger in DC accused her Uber driver of trying to choke her because she had been kissing her "white husband." The driver, on the other hand, claimed that the woman had been drunk, which caused her to behave aggressively towards him.[173] Upon investigation, it did appear that the driver's version of the story was closer to the truth. But what was telling about the incident was how Uber, specifically Kalanick, handled the situation.

After the altercation got reported in the media, Kalanick was quick to email the Uber press team and blame the media for making it appear that Uber was liable for such episodes. His message read in part, ". . . [W]e need to make sure that these writers don't come away thinking we are responsible, even when these things do go bad. . . . I think our statement goes most of the way there, but for whatever reason, these writers are starting to think that we are somehow liable for these incidents that aren't

---

[173] Caroline Moss, "Uber CEO Defends His Company after a Driver Is Accused of Assaulting a Passenger," Business Insider, September 16, 2013, https://www.businessinsider.com/ubers-ceo-travis-kalanick-defends-driver-in-assault-2013-9?IR=T.

even real in the first place."[174] In the article that revealed Kalanick's email contents, the reporter pointed out that Kalanick's "dismissiveness" was "troubling." In a significant way, it was a representation of the CEO's character and that character would much later jeopardize his standing in the very company he cofounded.

Several more incidents involving Uber drivers have been reported in the news throughout the years since the company began operations, but arguably the most disturbing concerned Jason Dalton, the man responsible for the Kalamazoo shootings in February 2016. In between Uber trip requests that he serviced, Dalton shot and killed six people and wounded two others.[175] According to Dalton, Uber was to blame for his behavior because it made him a "puppet". He had no previous criminal record or documented mental health issues. Although his lawyer wanted to file an insanity plea on his behalf, Dalton went against his lawyer's advice and pled

---

[174] Nitasha Tiku, "Uber CEO on Driver 'Assault': It's Not Real and We're Not Responsible," Valleywag, September 16, 2013, http://valleywag.gawker.com/uber-ceo-on-driver-assault-its-not-real-and-were-n-1323533057.

[175] Elisha Fieldstadt, "Michigan Uber Driver Jason Dalton Pleads Guilty in Kalamazoo Shooting Spree That Killed 6," NBC, January 7, 2019, https://www.nbcnews.com/news/us-news/michigan-uber-driver-jason-dalton-pleads-guilty-kalamazoo-shooting-spree-n955716.

guilty to all counts in January 2019. A month later, he was sentenced to life in prison without parole.[176]

The case focused attention on how Uber conducted security checks on their drivers, who are independent contractors and not employees.[177] According to a CNN investigation in 2018, both Uber and Lyft were found to have approved thousands of people as their drivers, who would have otherwise been disqualified for their previous criminal records.[178] While those were significant lapses in judgment on the part of Uber, it was conducting other far more "unusual" business practices that warranted even more attention.

Business Unusual

So, while Uber was dealing with many headaches caused by its drivers, it was also creating its own by not playing a fair game in its operations. For instance, one of the earliest

---

[176] Eric Levenson, "Uber Driver Who Killed 6 in Kalamazoo, Michigan, Shooting Rampage Sentenced to Life in Prison," CNN, February 5, 2019, https://edition.cnn.com/2019/02/05/us/uber-driver-killer-kalamazoo/index.html.
[177] *Ibid.*
[178] *Ibid.*

issues it made for itself and which persists to this day is the concept of surge pricing. It's actually not such a bad thing per se because it's a response to the law of supply and demand. Uber increases the ride price in certain places if there's a huge demand but not enough vehicles. It encourages drivers to go over to that area in order to service it.[179] And they get a premium for their efforts.

That in itself was not a problem, but at key moments when tragedies had struck certain cities, Uber's surge pricing appeared like a tone-deaf response to crises. It seemed like it was applied randomly and inconsistently. However, in an interview,[180] Kalanick clarified that they're not always able to see immediately what the cause of an upsurge demand is all about, but once they do, they switch the system off.

Many examples of inopportune times surge pricing kicked in abound online. Once, New York users bitterly complained on New Year's Eve of 2012 because the increase turned out to be from three to six times more than the regular

[179] Travis Kalanick, "Travis Kalanick Interview," Interview, The Late Show with Stephen Colbert, September 11, 2015, YouTube video, 5:54, https://www.youtube.com/watch?v=wGdjLv8neBs.
[180180] *Ibid.*

rate.[181] Then Hurricane Sandy happened in November 2012. While everybody else was getting on board to provide as much humanitarian help as they could to those affected by the rains and floods it caused, Uber came under fire again for doubling the prices. Because of the bitter criticism, the company was forced to roll back the prices to normal. Even so, they still continued to pay the drivers double for the trouble. Similar situations happened during the London and Sydney terror attacks. In both those and a few other circumstances, Uber apologized and made the appropriate amends.

Another business practice for which Uber was widely criticized was the "marketing" tactics it employed to get competitors' drivers to switch over to their side which came to light in January 2014.[182] Uber employees would request for rides from Gett, a rival company, and cancel their rides at the very last minute, thus depriving the competing driver of any income. It wasted not only the driver's gas, time, and energy, but it also kept legitimate Gett customers from availing of rides because drivers were preoccupied elsewhere. Top Uber executives were purportedly involved in the

---

[181] Taylor, "40."
[182] *Ibid*.

scheme, which was deemed too aggressive to say the least.[183]

It seemed rather odd that, in spite of the very obvious and unstoppable growth of Uber in the early years, some entities within Uber still felt that they had to employ dastardly tactics against its competitors. In August 2014, Uber was caught again employing similar time-wasting tactics on Lyft. It had even provided freelancer burner phones and credit cards to keep Lyft drivers busy with fake ride requests.[184]

In France, June 2015,[185] taxi drivers protested against what they felt was an unfair Uber strategy, when it fielded UberPOP, a low-cost type of ride. French cabbies were calling the company's practice "economic terrorism"

[183] Sam Biddle, "Uber's Dirty Trick Campaign against NYC Competition Came from the Top," Valleywag, January 24, 2014, http://valleywag.gawker.com/ubers-dirty-trick-campaign-against-nyc-competition-cam-1508280668.
[184] Caitlin McGarry, "Burner Phones and Cancelled Rides: How Uber Steals Drivers from Lyft," PC World, August 27, 2014, https://www.pcworld.com/article/2599506/burner-phones-and-canceled-rides-how-uber-steals-drivers-from-lyft.html.
[185] Rick Noack, "Anti-Uber Protests in France Lead to Scenes of Chaos and Violence," Washington Post, June 25, 2015, https://www.washingtonpost.com/news/worldviews/wp/2015/06/25/anti-uber-protests-in-france-lead-to-scenes-of-chaos-and-violence/?utm_term=.b4f3dc4e415c.

because it didn't create a level playing field for everyone. The term was especially in reference not only to Uber's low pricing but to the flexible hours of its drivers and the fact that it didn't quite follow the laws of the land when it came to public transportation providers. In the end, French courts ruled that the low-cost ride was detrimental to the industry, so UberPOP was discontinued.[186]

In January 2017, Uber was penalized and made to pay $20 million for misleading drivers about the amount of earnings they were to expect from working with the company.[187] The false claims were especially prevalent from late 2013 to 2015, during the time that Uber was actively recruiting Lyft drivers into its fold. In an official statement, it did reassure the public that it has improved the driver experience since that period, so everyone could expect smooth sailing in their dealings with the company.

---

[186] James Regan and John Irish, "France Cracks Down on Uber after Taxi Driver Protests," Reuters, June 25, 2015, https://www.reuters.com/article/us-france-uber-idUSKBN0P50RX20150625.
[187] Associated Press in San Francisco, "Uber to Pay $20M over Claims It Misled Drivers over How Much They Would Earn," *Guardian*, January 20, 2017, https://www.theguardian.com/technology/2017/jan/19/uber-settlement-ftc-driver-earnings-car-leases.

And these were just some of the more visible displays of unfair business practices exercised by Uber.

I Spy

Still related to its conduct of business, Uber had also committed some very serious breaches of privacy and security or have allowed them to happen on its unsuspecting users and drivers. For instance, back in November 2017,[188] it was reported that personal data from 57 million people had been compromised by hackers over a year ago, in October 2016. Kalanick found out about it a month after the incident, November 2016. In order to cover up the incident, Uber had paid the hackers $100,000 to delete the information they had stolen and never to speak about the incident. Everybody else found out about it 13 months after the fact! By then, Kalanick was no longer CEO, of course, so it was a headache that the new CEO, Dara Khosrowshahi, had to deal with. While it didn't seem like any of the data had actually been used, what scandalized people was that Uber did not

---

[188] Eric Newcomer, "Uber Paid Hackers to Delete Stolen Data on 57 Million People," Bloomberg, November 22, 2017, https://www.bloomberg.com/news/articles/2017-11-21/uber-concealed-cyberattack-that-exposed-57-million-people-s-data.

tell the public, especially their customers, immediately.

Another highly controversial privacy breach at Uber involved its "God View" tool. Back in November 2014, BuzzFeed reported that Uber had tracked one of its own editors by using the said tool.[189] It didn't just track cars, but it also made the driver's personal information visible to anyone with access to "God View." The investigation into this revelation resulted in Uber paying a $20,000 fine, removing any private data in the tracking system, and limiting the people who could access the tool. Uber also signed an "assurance of discontinuance," which essentially was a promise that it was not going to make its users' information publicly accessible.[190] Sadly, that didn't seem to be the case. Uber wasn't actually being compliant.

In October 2016, Samuel Ward Spangenberg, former forensic investigator of Uber, gave a

[189] Biz Carson, "Uber Settles Investigation into 'God View' Tool,'" Business Insider, January 6, 2016, https://www.businessinsider.com/uber-settles-investigation-into-god-view-tool-2016-1?IR=T.

[190] Elizabeth Bacharach, "Uber Has a 'God View' Tool and Was Allegedly Using It to Spy on Celebs," Cosmopolitan, December 14, 2016, https://www.cosmopolitan.com/lifestyle/a8495499/uber-using-god-view-tool-to-spy-on-celebs/.

testimony that seemed to imply that the tool was still active. It was still being used to track politicians, celebrities, and ex-partners. One of the most high-profile entertainers tracked appeared to have been Beyoncé.[191] Spangenberg's testimony came on the heels of his having been fired, supposedly from blowing the whistle on Uber's lack of adequate security. He was suing the company for its retaliation at his whistleblowing and its age discrimination against him.[192] Uber admitted that it had fired less than 10 people connected to the abuse of the "God View" tool, which by then was already renamed "Heaven View" but with the same functionality.

Another controversial tool Uber used was Greyball. A New York Times exposé revealed it was a program that collected data from the app "to identify and circumvent officials who were trying to clamp down on the ride-hailing service."[193] It was especially in use in cities like

---

[191] Alex Hern, "Uber Employees Spied on Ex-partners, Politicians, and Beyoncé," *Guardian*, December 13, 2016, https://www.theguardian.com/technology/2016/dec/13/uber-employees-spying-ex-partners-politicians-beyonce.

[192] *Ibid*.

[193] Mike Isaac, "How Uber Deceives the Authorities Worldwide," *New York Times*, March 3, 2017, https://www.nytimes.com/2017/03/03/technology/uber-greyball-program-evade-authorities.html.

Boston, Paris, and Las Vegas, and in countries like Australia, China, and South Korea.[194]

All these privacy and security breaches happened under Kalanick's watch. Goodness knows how many more were out there that no one even knew about. There seemed to be something rather strange going on in Uber and several more scandals put together shed a light into the inner workings of the organization, which became Kalanick's final undoing.

Kalanick's Chickens Come Home to Roost

Back in February 2014, a rather engaging, well-written feature article came out in GQ, written by Mickey Rapkin.[195] In it, he told of his one-week stint as an Uber driver and everything that he heard, smelled, and saw. The essay included a single paragraph that briefly profiled Kalanick. In full, it read this way (with very minimal stylistic editing):

"Every generation gets the app it deserves. Uber was cofounded by Travis Kalanick, a bro-y alpha nerd who's been coding since he was in sixth

---

[194] *Ibid*.

[195] Mickey Rapkin, "Uber Cab Confessions," *GQ*, February 27, 2014, https://www.gq.com/story/uber-cab-confessions.

grade and whose first brush with success came in the late 1990s, while he was still an undergrad at UCLA (that venture, called Scour, an early experiment in Napster-type file sharing—translation: file stealing—imploded in the face of a $250 billion copyright-infringement lawsuit). Not to make assumptions, but Kalanick probably wasn't the first kid in his class to lose his virginity. But the way he talks now—which is large—he's surely making up for lost time. When I tease him about his skyrocketing desirability, he deflects with a wisecrack about women on demand: yeah, we call that Boob-er."[196]

And with that single wisecrack, Kalanick set himself up for a barrage of criticism, focused mainly on the underlying misogyny and sexism of such a statement. In contrast, a month prior to the publication of the Rapkin piece, an online article appeared in Business Insider, written by Alyson Shontell,[197] which actually contained a statement in stark contrast to how Kalanick tried to present himself, that is, as a magnet to the ladies. Shontell wrote, "In recent years, Kalanick has been connected to a long line of beautiful brunettes. But he wasn't always a

[196] *Ibid.*
[197] Shontell, "Hail."

lady's man. A college friend said he 'had to grow into that.'"[198] For good or ill, it seemed that there was at least some veracity to the fact that Uber was an important factor to making the whole Kalanick persona attractive to women. Because prior to the power bestowed by the throne, Kalanick was just, well, Kalanick "the alpha nerd."

By the time Kalanick grew into his role as Uber CEO, there were already hints here and there that the corporate culture was going to look a lot like him or was already looking a lot like him. And that probably didn't mean that it looked like the boy you'd bring home to meet your parents and your furbaby poodle mix.

Remember that time Kalanick emailed his press team about how to handle a driver-versus-passenger controversy? You know, that one Valleywag leaked, where he sounded rather dismissive and arrogant about the whole incident. Well, that happened in September 2013, a few months before the Rapkin and Shontell articles came out in early 2014, so it is safe to say that Kalanick was already running things a little bit like his own, shall I call it, frat house.

---

[198] *Ibid.*

An article in Pando[199] explained to everyone why the one-paragraph Kalanick profile was just all sorts of squirmy and cringey things. A sentence in the Pando article read, "[M]aybe people talk about Uber in a douchey way because, when talking to journalists, the CEO of Uber says things that make him sound like a tremendous, unapologetic douche."[200] Carr, the article writer wasn't wrong at all. I mean, considering Kalanick was already the CEO of a billion-plus-dollar company, it is hard to dial back words like "boob-er," "somehow liable," "I would much rather be at the Shore Club," and "hashtag winning." For crying out loud, he was speaking to a journalist on the record, in his capacity as CEO. He wasn't the frat president at a spring-break kegger. And that was just the beginning of the scrutiny into the Uber corporate culture.

Then in October 2014, the Lyon office of Uber decided to partner with a "gentleman's website" called *Avions de Chasse*, for a special promo. Riders could request for free 20-minute rides

---

[199] Paul Bradley Carr, "'We Call That Boob-er:' The Four Most Awful Things Travis Kalanick Said in His GQ Profile," Pando, February 27, 2014, https://pando.com/2014/02/27/we-call-that-boob-er-the-four-most-awful-things-travis-kalanick-said-in-his-gq-profile/.
[200] Carr, "Four."

within city limits, driven around by "hot chicks."[201] A video that accompanied the promo left nothing to the imagination: high heels, lean calves, full cleavage, nubile skin, the works. The name of the website itself doesn't just translate to fighter jets but its colloquial meaning was an "incredibly hot chick."[202]

Before all signs of the promo were deleted and webpages scrubbed, BuzzFeed reported seeing sentences like "It's going to be the most beautiful thing on Earth" and "Who said women don't know how to drive?" associated to the promotion, on the site. *Avions de Chasse* founder, Pierre Garonnaire, said, "The goal was to start the promotion in Lyon and continue it in other cities in France. When Uber USA received information about it, they decided to cancel the operation because they don't like this kind of partnership, using these women."[203] He expressed disappointment but had no hard feelings about the whole thing. Disappointment, huh? Someone who wasn't

---

[201] Maya Kosoff, "An Uber Campaign That Promised to Pair Customers with 'Hot Chick' Drivers in France Has Been Scrubbed," Business Insider, October 23, 2014, https://www.businessinsider.com/uber-avions-de-chasse-promotion-with-hot-chick-drivers-2014-10?IR=T.
[202] *Ibid.*
[203] *Ibid.*

disappointed but rather enraged by the whole incident was Sarah Lacy, a book author and tech journalist.

Even before the "hot chicks" incident, Lacy had already written about the sexism and misogyny in Silicon Valley two weeks before it. In an article published on her own website,[204] Lacy called out the epicenter of the "tech startup ecosystem" for its "asshole" problem. Yes, it was about Silicon Valley misogyny, but it was especially about its hypocrisy. The bone of her contention was that venture capitalists weren't really investing in people and ideas as much as they were investing in assholes. Never mind that the people they were getting into bed with were never ever going to win a ribbon for best behavior. For as long as they could make money, preferably tons of it, then everybody should be good with that.

Lacy listed Uber in her roll call of assholes. She pointed out that at every step of its way, Uber was quick to flout regulations and the status quo in the markets it entered. Not too bad a thing per se. But its cavalier attitude also made it

---

[204] Sarah Lacy, "Venture Capital and the Great Big Silicon Valley Asshole Game," Pando, October 6, 2014, https://pando.com/2014/10/06/venture-capital-and-the-great-big-silicon-valley-asshole-game/.

overlook so many fundamentals like the background checks of its drivers. Uber was more concerned about how its story was being told than upholding the truth, even if it didn't make Uber too pretty at times. Earlier, I had mentioned the fact that Kalanick was a very good storyteller, always trying to take control of the narrative to make himself look good. Here was a journalist pretty much saying the same thing about Kalanick's baby. Very profound in all these discussions is the fact that Camp is never mentioned, even though he is as much a cofounder as Kalanick.

In looking back at some events in Uber's history, it is well worth recalling how Kalanick addressed the controversies that plagued the company, especially when it involved assaults, the rape, and other bad behavior. According to Lacy, Uber "vilified" riders when they accused its drivers of misdeeds, but Kalanick was also quick to belittle his own drivers when he couldn't wait for his self-driving experiment to come to fruition, so he could eliminate them.[205]

All this was just in the first article that Lacy wrote. When the "hot chicks" gaffe took place, she put Uber to task much more directly in her

---

[205] *Ibid.*

second piece. But before that happened, in the two-week intervening period between the two essays, a result of the original article was that Silicon Valley's venture capitalists came knocking on her door to thresh things out with her.[206] After all, she was herself a known entity among them. A few had even invested in her enterprise, the Pando website.

Nonetheless, Lacy came out of those discussions with more disgust than when she entered. While they understood her point about how oppressive Uber culture was towards women, as exemplified by the French promotion, and how permissive it was of bad boy behavior, with Kalanick leading the pack and calling his company "Boob-er" because of how it made him look more attractive to women drawn to his success, there was no real solution in sight. Uber investors needed the Kalanick types of this world to brave the continuous assault of enemies at its battlefronts.

Lacy believed that the Lyon office thought it was a good idea to launch such a campaign because there was an implicit permission and directive

---

[206] Sarah Lacy, "The Horrific Trickle Down of Asshole Culture: Why I've Just Deleted Uber from My Phone," Pando, October 22, 2014, https://pando.com/2014/10/22/the-horrific-trickle-down-of-asshole-culture-at-a-company-like-uber/.

issued by Kalanick in how they should market Uber.

"But the rapidly pulled post out of Uber Lyon proves what every CEO has always known: It's less about what you say directly and explicitly to employees that creates or destroys a culture. It's what they take from what you say. And I am not surprised that someone inside the company took Kalanick's callous attitude towards female riders and comments like "Boob-er" to mean that shocking level of exploitation and disrespect was appropriate—that it would even be celebrated by HQ.

"And like always, Uber has quietly withdrawn the offending post, but they won't apologize. That only exacerbates the internal message that this type of behavior was only bad because it wound up on BuzzFeed."[207]

As I mentioned before, a company does take the character of its founders, and Lacy calling out Kalanick and Uber about their uncouthness was really no surprise. Like father, like son. In the end, Lacy deleted the Uber app from her phone because she wanted nothing to do with such a company that didn't respect her or make her

---

[207] *Ibid.*

feel safe.[208] She felt that Uber needed to be held to a higher standard precisely because it offered services that transported sometimes vulnerable (intoxicated, disabled, sleeping, etc.) people to places even in the middle of the night. "Uber passengers are often locked, alone, late at night in a metal box with Uber drivers. Because of the service Uber offers as a company, the CEO and its investors need to go out of their way to set the tone that objectification of women is simply not acceptable."[209]

But the controversy didn't just lay to rest after that. Almost a month after the "hot chicks" episode and Lacy's rage at it, BuzzFeed's editor in chief, Ben Smith, reported that an Uber executive was thinking of digging up dirt on journalists like Lacy as a counterattack on them.[210] The Uber executive turned out to be Emil Michael, senior vice president of business.

In a dinner conversation that Michael believed was completely off the record, he voiced out his frustration at sensationalist media, which didn't

---

[208] *Ibid.*

[209] *Ibid.*

[210] Ben Smith, "Uber Executive Suggests Digging Up Dirt on Journalists," BuzzFeed, November 17, 2014, https://www.buzzfeednews.com/article/bensmith/uber-executive-suggests-digging-up-dirt-on-journalists#.yoNAxXY1m.

give a balanced perspective to their reporting. He was especially referring to Lacy's recent "attack" on Uber, where she accused the company of *ahem* misogyny and sexism *ahem*. He believed that her comments, including the accusation that Uber was working with a French escort service in that "hot chicks" promo, were over the top. He was incensed that, if other women followed her example by deleting their own Uber app from their phones, they were exposing themselves to the greater likelihood of being assaulted. There was a higher incidence of that happening among regular taxi drivers, after all, than among Uber drivers. And if that were ever to happen, God forbid, Michael felt that Lacy should be held directly accountable for the crimes committed against their person.

Michael vented further and suggested that Uber should hire researchers and opposition journalists to fight on Uber's behalf by digging up details about Lacy's and other journalists' private lives. The more salacious, the better would have been the likely directive had it been carried out. Except that it wasn't really issued as a directive. Michael was just as much a man enraged over dinner as Lacy was a woman enraged at the time she wrote her angry essays.

Michael had purportedly spoken those words while attending a private dinner hosted by Ian Osborne, an Uber consultant. Smith himself was there by invitation of Michael Wolff, a fellow journalist. Later, Wolff wrote about the incident. In it he explained that the Uber executive was under the impression that the function was completely off the record. Wolff admitted that it was his failing that he had forgotten to inform Smith about it.[211] According to other guests at that dinner, Smith had indeed painted a very erroneous picture of the incident. And mind you, what a roster of dinner guests that was: Travis Kalanick, the actor Ed Norton, film producer Shauna Robertson, *Daily News* owner Mort Zuckerman, Huffington Post chief Arianna Huffington, and a few more. Not many were on the same page as Smith was in the way the dinner conversation and ambience were painted. But the damage had already been done to all parties concerned.

To his credit, Michael issued a public apology and clarified that he never spoke on behalf of Uber. He owned his careless statements and

---

[211] Michael Wolff, "Wolff: Behind the Scenes at Uber/BuzzFeed Fracas," USA Today, November 19, 2014, https://www.usatoday.com/story/money/columnist/wolff/2014/11/19/behind-the-scenes-uber-buzzfeed-fracas/19269737/.

admitted that it was his frustration that led to all that was said, not any malice or vindictiveness. And definitely, nothing that represented the official stance of Uber itself.[212] In this particular controversy, although Kalanick was also present at the dinner, it was just Michael who came into public view to bite the bullet, so to speak.

Nonetheless, there were other things brewing underneath the surface that would soon put to question so much about the corporate culture in Uber that would imperil the positions of several executives, including Michael and even Kalanick himself. And much of them were related to the subject matter that Lacy had protested about in her aforementioned articles.

You and I can take a deep breath here and survey where we are at now in terms of the Uber narrative. Take note that, at this point, in the year 2014, we are just three years away from when the #metoo movement went viral in October 2017. That was when sexual harassment accusations against the Hollywood

---

[212] Alex Hern, "Uber Executive Apologizes after Suggesting the Firm Dig Dirt on Hostile Journalists," *Guardian*, November 18, 2019, https://www.theguardian.com/technology/2014/nov/18/uber-exec-apologises-emil-michael-journalist-sarah-lacy.

mogul Harvey Weinstein first came to light. Along the way, leading up to that moment, sentiments were already stirring about how corporate cultures needed to change because of their unfair and oppressive treatment of women. Perhaps, top executives now needed to be held more accountable for their actions. That was what we saw when Lacy took on the Kalanicks and Ubers of the world.

And now the story was starting to turn. As it was, Silicon Valley was already not the most gender-balanced workplace in the world.[213] Throwing in random, politically incorrect, and unsound remarks as Michael's or even Kalanick's "Boob-er" only served to push women away from the tech world, even though their ranks were filled with so many competent, highly qualified engineers, developers, analysts, mathematicians, and more, who could more than go head-to-head with the best of men.

Maybe, a new awareness was beginning or needed to emerge in viewing the likes of Kalanick. His way wasn't the only way to do business in Silicon Valley. As the head of a very

[213] Lydia Dallett, "This One Stat Shows Just How Far behind Silicon Valley Is on Gender Equality," Business Insider, February 4, 2014, https://www.businessinsider.com/silicon-valley-and-gender-equality-twitter-2014-2?IR=T.

prominent global tech company, he had to measure up to a higher standard than everybody else. While his aggressiveness may have been welcome in corporate boardrooms because it sealed deals, shut down the competition, and minted money, it was not necessarily the best to have it on display everywhere else. It was time to re-view Travis Kalanick and his brand of leadership.

Chapter 6: This Is Where the Trip Ends

#DeleteUber Woes

Let us fast forward to the year 2017, when everything unraveled for Kalanick and Uber. That year started out quite badly for the pair because the #DeleteUber campaign went viral. That wasn't exactly how anybody would have started their January, right? But that's how everything went down. And down was the prevalent direction for Kalanick's journey that year.

The crusade had kicked off because many people thought that Uber took advantage of a very politically charged situation to make a profit. First, the scene was set when US President Donald Trump issued a travel ban against seven predominantly Muslim countries: Iraq, Syria, Iran, Libya, Somalia, Yemen, and Sudan.[214] Although Trump himself reiterated several times that it was not a ban based on religion but on potential terrorist activity, the

---

[214] "Trump's Executive Order: Who Does Travel Ban Affect?" BBC, February 10, 2017, https://www.bbc.com/news/world-us-canada-38781302.

general public and the media were quick to create the #MuslimBan hashtag to protest against the perceived prejudices of the administration.

Like wildfire, the rally spread and several people congregated around airports to convey their support of those affected. New York taxi workers also took a stand and expressed their solidarity by not plying the airport route for at least an hour. In response to the call for a strike, the official Uber Twitter account tweeted that surge pricing had been turned off in the general vicinity of JFK. Users could expect longer wait times, so the company urged for patience all around.[215]

People read the Uber tweet as a form of strike-breaking because it encouraged its drivers to continue their business. If its competitor was not on the streets, then Uber drivers had free rein to go to the airport and to pick up a high volume of passengers waiting to be serviced. It felt like an exploitative move and Uber users would have nothing to do with the scabby company. #DeleteUber very quickly trended in

[215] German Lopez, "Why People Are Deleting Uber from Their Phones after Trump's Executive Order," Vox, January 29, 2017, https://www.vox.com/policy-and-politics/2017/1/29/14431246/uber-trump-muslim-ban.

social media, accompanied by screenshots of the popup window for the delete action. In a single weekend, Uber lost about 200,000 accounts.[216] Supposedly, the total eventually came up to 500,000.[217] Many of those who uninstalled the app from their phones vowed never to return to Uber and to use Lyft only forevermore. Lyft's own response to the crisis was to donate $1 million to the American Civil Liberties Union over the next four years "to defend the constitution."[218]

To counter the anti-Uber campaign and people's wrong perception about Uber's position regarding Trump's travel ban, Kalanick posted on his personal Facebook page (and tweeted the same) that Uber was going to provide legal support to its drivers from the banned countries, who had left the US on holiday and could not return in the next 90 days because of Trump's directive. The company was also going to compensate them for lost wages. Furthermore, he promised to mobilize a lobby for the dissolution of the ban. He was going to

---

[216] Taylor, "40."

[217] Levin, "Uber's."

[218] Elena Cresci, "#DeleteUber: How Social Media Turned on Uber," *Guardian*, January 30, 2017, https://www.theguardian.com/technology/2017/jan/30/deleteuber-how-social-media-turned-on-uber.

ensure that there would be a legal fund for Uber drivers, complete with translation services.[219]

Besides Kalanick's personal posts, an official statement from Uber clarified the controversial tweet: "We wanted people to know they could use Uber to get to and from JFK at normal prices."[220] I actually agree with Uber on this one. It did look like they simply wanted people to know that a premium charge was not in play for them to have access to transportation. However, I also couldn't blame the general public for the swift and retaliatory action it meted on Uber because there was precedence for Uber's bad behavior. There were many previous instances of the company's tone-deafness. I had mentioned a few in previous chapters: London. Sydney. Hurricane Sandy. People did not see Uber's intentions very clearly perhaps because their minds were already clouded by all those previous incidents. I couldn't blame them at all. Besides, even before the misunderstood tweet, people already had a different reason for uninstalling Uber from their phones.

A month before the immigration ban, in December 2016, Kalanick took on a role in the

---

[219] Cresci, "#DeleteUber."

[220] *Ibid*.

new Trump administration. He joined other business leaders to become a part of the new president's economic advisory council. Many Uber users remembered that and included it as one of the reasons why they were deleting their Uber accounts. They didn't want to have anything to do with a company ran by a person allied with Trump.

As the clamor for an Uber boycott continued and escalated, Kalanick finally had to step down from the council. He wrote an email to Uber staff: "Joining the group was not meant to be an endorsement of the president or his agenda but unfortunately it has been misinterpreted to be exactly that."[221] Much later, people found out that he just really wanted a seat at the table beside Elon Musk and other business leaders.[222]

His explanation sounded almost like his ego talking. He should have anticipated that people

[221] Julia Carrie Wong, "Uber CEO Steps Down from Trump Advisory Council after Users Boycott," *Guardian*, February 3, 2017, https://www.theguardian.com/technology/2017/feb/02/travis-kalanick-delete-uber-leaves-trump-council.

[222] Eric Newcomer and Brad Stone, "The Fall of Travis Kalanick Was a Lot Weirder and Darker Than You Thought," *Bloomberg Businessweek*, January 18, 2018, https://www.bloomberg.com/news/features/2018-01-18/the-fall-of-travis-kalanick-was-a-lot-weirder-and-darker-than-you-thought.

were not going to see his role to be anything other than a form of collusion. You don't join a group that you don't somehow identify with. Something about birds, feathers, and flocking. Considering how Kalanick had always shown himself to take contrary stands about many things (reference here his constant fights with taxi regulators and all) and do so consistently, many people did wonder why he didn't do the same for the council invite. It was a simple equation in the minds of many former Uber users. If you're not there as a sign of approval, why are you there at all? And that's why people flew the coop. They weren't about to sanction the seemingly self-serving political maneuverings of Kalanick. If you disagree, you flee.

In addition, Kalanick is or was a self-proclaimed fan of Ayn Rand,[223] the philosopher who popularized objectivism and the virtue of selfishness—the best friend of many of the world's capitalists. If Kalanick was not a Trump advocate, he could have and should have taken a principled stand against joining the economic

[223] Maya Kosoff, "Everything You Need to Know about 'The Fountainhead,' a Book That Inspires Billionaire Uber CEO Travis Kalanick," Business Insider, June 1, 2015, https://www.businessinsider.com/how-ayn-rand-inspired-uber-ceo-travis-kalanick-2015-6?IR=T.

advisory council because it would have been the Howard Roark thing to do.

Susan Fowler's Blog Post

Before February 2017, the general public did not know who Susan Fowler was. I certainly hadn't heard of her. And I'm sure that prior to that month, she maintained her status as a private citizen. I don't know about you, but I'm personally not a big fan of being in the limelight. I don't even like taking selfies. I'd much rather curl up in a corner and read a book with a cup of steaming hot java beside me.

So what thrust Fowler quite suddenly into the center of so much public scrutiny? She did a simple thing: she published a post on her blog.[224] It wasn't just any regular post about a joke shared by a friend or a lovely weekend up at Lake Tahoe. It was a detailed narrative of her roughly 13-month stint at Uber as a Site Reliability Engineer (SRE), and it wasn't just about software and infrastructure and operations, it was pretty much a tell-all of the sexual harassment, sexism, and misogyny she

---

[224] Susan Fowler, "Reflecting on One Very, Very Strange Year at Uber," *Susan J. Fowler* (blog), February 19, 2017, https://www.susanjfowler.com/blog/2017/2/19/reflecting-on-one-very-strange-year-at-uber.

and a bunch of other women experienced at Uber. And how they reported their experiences to HR. And how HR stood with managers to cover things up. It was explosive.

One of Fowler's first experiences of sexual harassment at Uber involved a manager who propositioned her for sex. When she reported him to HR, nothing was done about her complaint because he was a high performer in the company,[225] meaning, he received stellar reviews from his superiors.

She also wrote about how her particular part of the organization boasted of 25% women. By the time she left, however, it had gone down to just six percent. Something as (almost) trivial as a promised leather jacket became a demonstration of the gender disparity. Uber refused to buy the women their jackets simply because they were too few and didn't warrant a discount from the jacket supplier to make a purchase worthwhile.[226] Yeah. Let that sink in for a minute.

As soon as the blog gained traction and caught the attention of Uber execs, there was a mad scramble for the door, the hills, anywhere but

[225] Taylor, "40."
[226] Fowler, "Reflecting."

Uber HQ. The shit was about to hit the fan. Even Uber users participated by doing a second wave of #DeleteUber.[227] Without a doubt, at the back of everybody's minds, they knew heads were going to roll. Kalanick called for an internal investigation into the allegations made by Fowler.[228] He had Arianna Huffington, not just the HuffPost chief but also an Uber board member, and Eric H. Holder Jr., former attorney general of the United States of America under President Barack Obama, lead the probe.

While Kalanick did his best to live up to his corporate title at that time of crisis, a *New York Times* article was quick to point out that it was his very character that was reflected in the current, troublesome internal culture of his company. "As chief executive, Mr. Kalanick has long set the tone for Uber. Under him, Uber has taken a pugnacious approach to business, flouting local laws and criticizing competitors in a race to expand as quickly as possible. Mr. Kalanick, 40, has made pointed displays of ego:

---

[227] Johana Bhuiyan, "Everything You Need to Know about Uber's Turbulent 2017," Recode, August 20, 2017, https://www.recode.net/2017/8/20/16164176/uber-2017-timeline-scandal.

[228] Mike Isaac, "Inside Uber's Aggressive, Unrestrained Workplace Culture," *New York Times*, February 22, 2017, https://www.nytimes.com/2017/02/22/technology/uber-workplace-culture.html?smid=tw-share&_r=0.

in a GQ article in 2014, he referred to Uber as 'Boob-er' because of how the company helped him attract women."[229] Essentially, the article was implying that Kalanick was really to blame for how people ran the show within Uber. He himself had set the tone and example for them to follow.

When Huffington and Holder took on their new temporary roles as internal investigators, not everybody thought it was a good idea because they both had vested interests in the company. Huffington was a board member and Holder was a retained advocate for some Uber legal matters. The two people who voiced their dissent over the dual appointments were Mitch Kapor and Freada Kapor Klein.[230] They themselves had stakes in the company as early investors, but they were vocal about their objections because they knew something was terribly wrong, "toxic" even, with Uber and its leadership, and that needed to change. "To us, this decision is yet another example of Uber's continued unwillingness to be open, transparent, and direct."[231] They wanted impartial findings.

---

[229] *Ibid.*
[230] Bhuiyan, "Everything."
[231] *Ibid.*

As it turned out, Fowler's revelations were just skimming the surface of what had become a vulgar corporate culture. More salacious details came to the fore in the NYT article. For instance, in a Las Vegas global meeting, where Beyoncé was the main entertainment, many employees were seen using cocaine and many female employees got groped.[232] With those two descriptions alone, you would think it was Panama City Beach during spring break. Sure, within 24 hours, one manager was fired for the latter transgression, but that was the only disciplinary action reported in the NYT, stemming from that function.

You can say that the Fowler post was a tipping point for Uber. The time for it finally to clean house had come. Possibly the first casualty was Amit Singhal, senior vice president of engineering, who was advised to resign. Although he had just joined Uber, he needed to leave the company because he had failed to disclose sexual harassment accusations leveled at him when he was still working at Google. He denied all of it, of course, but he still needed to leave anyway.[233]

---

[232] Isaac, "Inside."
[233] Katie Reilly, "Every Event That Led to Uber CEO Travis Kalanick's Resignation," *Fortune*, June 21, 2017,

And then a new Kalanick scandal surfaced. While out and about with friends on Super Bowl weekend that year, Kalanick jumped into an Uber, and he and his party were taken to their destination. The driver knew it was the CEO himself, so just before Kalanick alighted, the driver engaged him in a conversation. He expressed his dissatisfaction at the losses he was incurring because of UberX. His income had become much smaller, making it more difficult for him to earn a decent living.[234] Instead of just reflecting on the driver's words, Kalanick began an argument with him. The CEO pointed out that the driver was not taking responsibility for his own failures, before leaving the shaken guy alone in his car. The driver made sure to give Kalanick a one-star rating as a passenger.[235]

When Bloomberg aired the video, Kalanick was stunned and brought to his knees.[236] In an email to Uber staff, Kalanick said, "My job as your

http://fortune.com/2017/06/21/uber-controversy-timeline-travis-kalanick/.

[234] Julia Carrie Wong, "Uber CEO Travis Kalanick Caught on Video Arguing with Driver about Fares," Guardian, March 1, 2017, https://www.theguardian.com/technology/2017/feb/28/uber-ceo-travis-kalanick-driver-argument-video-fare-prices.

[235] Ibid.

[236] Newcomer and Stone, "Fall."

leader is to lead . . . and that starts with behaving in a way that makes us all proud. That is not what I did and it cannot be explained away. This is the first time I've been willing to admit that I need leadership help and I intend to get it."[237] It was a rare moment for Kalanick to show his underbelly. But that vulnerability didn't last long.

Kalanick's proposal to make peace with the driver, Fawzi Kamel, was to meet him at some Switzerland-type of place, where they could talk privately for about five minutes and then move on. It didn't quite go as scripted. Instead of just a few minutes, he and Kamel debated again for over an hour over the same issue, Uber's pricing policies. By the time their argument winded down, Kalanick was thinking of giving the driver some Uber stock, which unnerved Wayne Ting, who ran the San Francisco business and was there in the room when it happened. Ting thought it financially irresponsible of Kalanick, as it would set a precedent for Uber needing to compensate everyone who felt mistreated by it or by its CEO. Uber lawyers refused to allow the deal to cover for Kalanick's personal misdeeds, so Kalanick ended up paying Kamel $200,000

---

[237] Wong, "Caught."

from his own pocket.[238]

Clearly, the tide was turning. Evidence kept piling up, questioning his suitability and credibility to lead Uber. And there was more.

Uber Execs Visit an Escort/Karaoke Bar on a Work Trip

"More" turned out to be another scandalous partying a la Vegas, this time in Seoul back in 2014. The story source turned out to be Kalanick's ex, Gabi Holzwarth.[239] At that bar, customers could call out the women's tag numbers and they could spend the evening together, singing their hearts out. At the end of the night and presumably for the right price, the ladies could also "go home" with the customers. The Uber party that went to that bar that night included Holzwarth, Kalanick, a female marketing manager, and four male executives.[240]

---

[238] Newcomer and Stone, "Fall."
[239] Alex Hern, "Uber Execs Including Travis Kalanick Went to Escort/Karaoke Bar," *Guardian*, March 27, 2017, https://www.theguardian.com/technology/2017/mar/27/uber-execs-including-travis-kalanick-went-to-escortkaraoke-bar.
[240] Amir Efrati, "Uber Group's Visit to Seoul Escort Bar Sparked HR Complaint," Information, March 24, 2017,

The whole setup did not sit well with the marketing manager and she left just a few minutes after the four male colleagues made their choices. Holzwarth and Kalanick didn't stay long either. They left after about 45 minutes to an hour. However short she had stayed at the bar, it was enough of an unpleasant experience for the marketing manager to file a complaint with HR.[241]

The three-year-old story would have died a natural death, except that Holzwarth felt compelled to publicize it around the time of the Huffington-Holder investigations. She had received a phone call from Kalanick's Michael, reminding her to tell anyone who asked about their 2014 trip that they all had nothing but a good time at the bar.[242] His message felt vaguely ominous to her and she didn't want to be manipulated or intimidated into silence, hence, her aired version of the event.[243]

When interviewed, Michael admitted to the phone call but denied it was nothing more than just a heads-up from him for her to expect the

---

https://www.theinformation.com/articles/uber-groups-visit-to-seoul-escort-bar-sparked-hr-complaint.
[241] Efrati, "Uber."
[242] Hern, "Escort."
[243] Efrati, "Uber."

media. "Given the intense news cycle, I thought it was the right thing to do to reach out and let her know that reporters may try to contact her directly. I have known her for a long time, consider her a friend, and did not want her to be taken by surprise. Her recollection of this conversation was different from mine and I am very sorry if the purpose of my call was misunderstood."[244]

She said. He said. Regardless of all that, what was clear in the event and its post-scenario was that members of the highest ranks in Uber (mostly men, of course) were running roughshod all over the place and no one was stopping them. Holzwarth described Kalanick as "part of a class of privileged men who have been taught they can do whatever they want and now they can."[245] In the post-Fowler situation, her description of Kalanick could very well apply to many of the male executives in the company.

Unfond Farewells

Misfortunes continued to plague Uber as the first quarter of 2017 winded down. One involved

_____

[244] *Ibid.*
[245] *Ibid.*

Ed Baker, vice president of product and growth, who resigned with this official statement: "I have always wanted to apply my experience in technology and growth to the public sector. And now seems like the right moment to get involved."[246] However, it appeared as though his departure was actually triggered by an allegation of sexual misconduct against him.[247]

Shortly after Baker's resignation, Jeff Jones followed suit. His departure was especially significant because he was the president of Uber, a position he had held for only the past seven months.[248] His own statement was very unequivocal in relation to the ongoing investigations: "It is now clear, however, that the beliefs and approach to leadership that have guided my career are inconsistent with what I saw and experienced at Uber, and I can no longer continue as president of the ride-sharing business."[249]

Almost a year after Jones's resignation, Bloomberg published an article that included a

---

[246] Bhuiyan, "Everything."

[247] Kara Swisher and Johana Bhuiyan, "Uber's VP of Product and Growth Ed Baker Has Resigned," Recode, March 3, 2017, https://www.recode.net/2017/3/3/14805384/uber-ed-baker-resigns-travis-kalanick.

[248] Reilly, "Every."

[249] Ibid.

peek into that controversial departure. "In exit interviews with Uber board members, [Jones] was more specific, excoriating Kalanick's shotgun management style and unwillingness to listen. [He] seemed so eager to leave the company that he declined to negotiate an exit package, potentially leaving millions of dollars behind."[250] With Jones's resignation, it seemed even more imperative for Kalanick to find a COO, but all he was coming up with was a huge bag of nothing.

About two and a half months after Jones left, the top finance guy of Uber, Gautam Gupta, also tendered his resignation, explaining that he planned to join another startup.[251] It seemed to be an amicable parting of ways between him and Uber, so nothing much was said about it, except that it left a gaping hole in the organization. Now, Uber had to look for both a COO and a CFO to complete its management team. Gupta himself was just head of finance but the highest-ranking finance officer.

Just a few days after Gupta's resignation, one

[250] Newcomer and Stone, "Fall."
[251] Johana Bhuiyan, "Uber's Head of Finance Has Left the Company," Recode, May 31, 2017, https://www.recode.net/2017/5/31/15722452/uber-finance-gautam-gupta-departure.

manager's head did roll. Eric Alexander was the president of business in Uber's Asia-Pacific region.[252] He was also the man responsible for obtaining the Indian rape victim's medical records a few years ago, the one whose story I told you about in another chapter. Alexander had shown the said documents around to Kalanick, Michael, and a few others within Uber, as they discussed ways to discredit the survivor.

On June 8, 2017, a day after Alexander's firing, another nail was driven into Kalanick's casket, when a company-wide email from the CEO was published online. The contents were ground rules meant to cover everyone's behavior during a Miami company retreat way back in 2013. That in itself sounded innocuous enough. But then, the email happened to have been written in true Kalanick bro style.[253] In one section, Kalanick wrote, verbatim:

"Do not have sex with another employee UNLESS a) you have asked that person for that

[252] Bhuiyan, "Everything."

[253] Kara Swisher and Johana Bhuiyan, "Uber CEO Kalanick Advised Employees on Sex Rules for a Company Celebration in 2013 'Miami Letter,'" Recode, June 8, 2017, https://www.recode.net/2017/6/8/15765514/2013-miami-letter-uber-ceo-kalanick-employees-sex-rules-company-celebration.

privilege and they have responded with an emphatic 'YES! I will have sex with you' AND b) the two (or more) of you do not work in the same chain of command. Yes, that means that Travis will be celibate on this trip. #CEOLife #FML."[254]

Against the backdrop of Lacy's and Fowler's and goodness-knows-who-else's assertions and revelations about the Silicon Valley corporate culture, specifically Uber's, the email bombshell seemed the fitting but tragic cap to Holder's investigations. Everything boiled down to this: the CEO of one of the highest-valued tech companies in the world sounded just like your everyday bro and he wanted you to know that he wasn't getting any at the upcoming family picnic because he was on babysitting duties. #FML indeed.

Eric Holder's Uber Report

Three days after Kalanick's email was published, Holder's report came out and Uber's board of directors unanimously voted to implement all his recommendations.[255] The report was 13 pages long and covered four

[254] *Ibid*.
[255] Reilly, "Every."

overarching themes:[256] 1. Tone at the top, 2. Trust, 3. Transformation, and 4. Accountability.

Holder's findings were clear in that Kalanick had had too much power too long and needed many of his responsibilities to be delegated to a chief operating officer who was to be Kalanick's full partner. There was to be no more of the heavy-handed, one-sided leadership style that characterized Kalanick's. Harping back on Lacy's articles, the asshole leader was no longer to be tolerated.

In retrospect, when the Silicon Valley venture capitalists told Lacy that time that we all needed the Kalanicks to run the world, regardless of their asshole and douchebag personas, they weren't doing anyone any favors, including themselves. At some point, something would have had to give because there's always an expiry date for the tolerance anyone can accord that sort of behavior. It was just way too toxic for anyone to withstand. Kapor and Kapor Klein had understood that.

Now, in response to Fowler's case, Holder

[256] Polina Marinova, "10 Things You Need to Know from Eric Holder's Uber Report," *Fortune*, June 13, 2017, http://fortune.com/2017/06/13/uber-internal-investigation-results-public/.

recommended that "substantiated complaints of discrimination and harassment,"[257] had to be given their full day in court. No one was going to be immune from discipline, even if he or she was a valuable member of the organization based on performance. If Uber were to run truly as a company that promoted its employees based on merit, then every aspect of their conduct within corporate boundaries and campuses had to be unassailable. It was the company's responsibility to ensure that its employees knew that they were seen and that they were heard. Really, it was all about basic human respect. And they were not going to be punished for simply speaking out the truth.

Because there was not enough diversity (gender, racial, or otherwise) at Uber, Holder went on to endorse that the head of diversity should be made more visible and that a "diversity advisory board" needed to be established.[258] Uber was also henceforth expected to publish its diversity statistics regularly. It was a concrete way of checking that the company was meeting its goals or was at least working towards it.

When Uber came out with its first-ever diversity

---

[257] *Ibid.*

[258] *Ibid.*

report back in March 2017, there were no nasty surprises. Its numbers mirrored the same ones you'd expect and find across pretty much most, if not all, companies in America and elsewhere. In a nutshell: its human resources were mostly white and Asian. And male.[259] It was definitely time to stir things up in that department.

It's always very interesting to note how the corporate world can be quick to adapt to the latest technologies, the newest business models, the most advanced flow systems, and so on and so forth, but be very slow to embrace sociocultural and/or sociopolitical transformations. Uber would have been the perfect showcase of such a change. It was supposed to be in its DNA to welcome the new, to disrupt the status quo, to allow for a truly diverse organization. Instead, it fell back on the traditional ways of doing things. But now Holder's report and recommendations were going to keep it on its toes.

Holder's report also focused on what to do with Uber leadership. A greater degree of

---

[259] Deirdre Bosa, "Uber Releases Its First Diversity Report—and It Looks Like Pretty Much Every Other Tech Company," CNBC, March 28, 2017, https://www.cnbc.com/2017/03/28/uber-diversity-report-released.html.

accountability was now to be required of senior executives. Their performance had to show that they were being responsive to the company's diversity goals, employee complaints, employee satisfaction, and compliance.[260] It was no longer going to be enough that they finished projects on time and under budget or whatever metrics there were in place before. This was a recommendation that safeguarded the integrity of governance. It was in answer to the constant but often unspoken question, *"Quis custodiet ipsos custodes?"* Indeed, who was responsible for guarding the guardians? Holder and his team had now created a viable solution to the conundrum.

Some pragmatic suggestions from the Holder team included additional independent board seats for oversight of Uber management and mandatory leadership coaching.[261] A few more covered human resource matters. HR had to cast a broader net in bringing in talents to Uber. It had to do some serious catching up on its diversity goals by applying the Rooney rule:[262] at least one woman and one underrepresented minority should be considered for any position.

---

[260] Marinova, "10."
[261] *Ibid*.
[262] *Wikipedia*, s.v. "Rooney Rule," accessed March 11, 2019, https://en.wikipedia.org/wiki/Rooney_Rule.

HR also had to discourage romantic relationships between bosses and direct subordinates because it created all sorts of ethical and moral headaches. Holder also recommended for a review of pay practices.[263]

Shortly before the Holder report came out, the biggest earth-shaking news was announced: Uber had fired 20 of its employees as a result of the investigations in the past few months. They had been done quietly and discreetly behind the scenes. The primary reasons for their sacking were harassment, discrimination, and inappropriate behavior.[264] While no names were leaked or revealed, an unnamed employee confirmed that the number included top managers. The day after the Holder recommendations were unanimously approved by the Uber board, Emil Michael resigned from his post as senior vice president.[265] Although nothing specific was said about why, there were indications that his resignation was related to

---

[263] Marinova, "10."

[264] Mike Isaac, "Uber Fires 20 amid Investigation into Workplace Culture," *New York Times*, June 6, 2017, https://www.nytimes.com/2017/06/06/technology/uber-fired.html.

[265] Johana Bhuiyan, "Uber's SVP of Business Emil Michael Has Left the Company," Recode, June 12, 2017, https://www.recode.net/2017/6/12/15783204/uber-emil-michael-step-down-resign.

the investigations done on the corporate culture of Uber.

At this point, you can say that Uber was coming to a crossroad. It had been a great ride up to that point with Kalanick behind the wheel because it was his aggressiveness, cavalier attitude, and overriding hubris that helped make Uber into a (at that time) $70 billion leviathan of a logistics company. However, it was also those very qualities that had almost caused the company to tumble down the precipice. If there was anything to see and to learn from the first six months of 2017, it was that Uber had become too big for its own shoes. It couldn't take correction. It wouldn't listen to reason. It didn't welcome adult supervision. In short, it sounded a lot like Kalanick.

So with the bad apples thrown away, the next step Uber had to do, of course, was to hire new people. Frances Frei, a Harvard Business School professor, and management consultant, came in as the first senior vice president for leadership and strategy.[266] Then it also hired Bozoma St. John, formerly of Apple, who came on board as the new chief brand officer.[267]

---

[266] *Ibid.*
[267] *Ibid.*

The foremost job that had yet to be filled, of course, was that of the chief operating officer. Since Kalanick's start of the search sometime in March,[268] he still hadn't found a suitable candidate three months down the road. Unknown to him, however, there was about to be another vacancy at Uber and it was not going to be to his liking.

A Permanent Leave of Absence

Kalanick's mother died towards the end of May in a freak accident when her boat hit a rock and began to sink. She was with her husband when it happened. He survived. She did not. But they were both found ashore near where the mishap occurred.[269] Everybody who knew Kalanick knew that he was close to his parents, so his mom's death was likely to devastate to him. And it did. It was devastating enough for him to contemplate an indefinite leave of absence from Uber. Quite an unprecedented thought.

In the middle of Kalanick's personal tragedy, he still had to deal with the turmoil going on in the

---

[268] Bhuiyan, "Everything."
[269] "Uber Boss Travis Kalanick's Mother Dies in Boating Accident," *Guardian*, May 28, 2017, https://www.theguardian.com/technology/2017/may/28/uber-boss-travis-kalanicks-mother-dies-in-boating-accident.

war room. Holder's recommendations all pointed to one thing: Uber had to change. And so did its leaders. Already, leadership changes had begun as some resigned from their posts, while others got themselves fired. Kalanick knew he too needed to change, judging by his meltdown inside an Uber vehicle. He needed to grow up. And fast.

That realization must have been quite a feat for Kalanick. Previously, whenever anything negative was said in public about Uber or him, his fallback was to blame it as a public-relations issue, not a cultural one.[270] I understood where he was coming from. Don't forget that, early on, I had told you that Kalanick was really a master storyteller. If he considered anything a PR problem and not otherwise, it was probably because he was viewing it simply as a tale told wrong. If the narrative could be framed it a better way, maybe people wouldn't be ganging up on him and his company.

But this time, things were different. So Kalanick did what needed to be done. On June 13, 2017, he announced his intention to go on an indefinite leave of absence from Uber, leaving 16 executives to take charge of daily

---

[270] Newcomer and Stone, "Fall."

management and to fulfill sweeping institutional and operational changes. He was clear in an email circulated among employees that his reason was primarily so he could mourn the death of his mom. And so he could also work on Travis 2.0.[271] The day before his announcement, the board had been in an all-day meeting, discussing an agenda resulting from Holder's report and recommendations. It was also the same day that Emil Michael resigned from Uber and Wan Ling Martello was appointed to the Uber board as a member[272]— yes, to that independent seat Holder recommended. So far so good, right?

Let me backtrack just a bit regarding Michael's resignation. It was an event that needed to happen because of a clamor growing within Uber's Executive Leadership Team itself. Six members had even sent a confidential letter to the board, requesting for the appointment of an independent board chairman, Michael's sacking, and Kalanick's leave of absence.[273] There was so much political maneuvering

[271] "Uber CEO Travis Kalanick Will Take Indefinite Leave of Absence," Reuters, June 13, 2017, http://fortune.com/2017/06/13/uber-ceo-travis-kalanick-leave-of-absence/.
[272] Bhuiyan, "Everything."
[273] Newcomer and Stone, "Fall."

happening in the shadows, I tell you.

And then on the same day that Kalanick announced his indefinite leave, David Bonderman, Uber board member and a founder of private equity firm TPG Capital, which is one of Uber's investors, stepped down from his role on the board because of a sexist remark he had made during a meeting that day.[274]

In that meeting, Huffington had said, "There's a lot of data that shows, when there's one woman on the board, it's much more likely that there will be a second woman on the board." Bonderman countered, "Actually, what it shows is that it's much more likely to be more talking."[275] You be the judge how that sounded like. If it was meant as a wisecrack, it certainly was a 'crack heard round the world' by the end of the business day.

Even while Kalanick was supposed to be on leave, he was still very much present in conference calls and the recruitment of people to fill vacant executive positions. He also continued to review the company's internal

---

[274] Heather Somerville, "Uber Director David Bonderman Resigns from Board Following Comment about Women," Reuters, June 14, 2017, https://www.reuters.com/article/us-uber-bonderman-idUSKBN195053.
[275] Somerville, "Bonderman."

data. Uber's finance team was supposedly spreading the word that Kalanick was still in control. In his absence, executives and board members suspected that Huffington was his proxy.[276] All this was probably what led to the next events.

Apparently, Kalanick's indefinite leave was truly not enough for a significant number of investors. It had been repeatedly pointed out that Uber's workplace and corporate cultures were the way they were because of Kalanick's leadership. Just reference everything that Holder recommended and read between the lines. Kalanick was able to take Uber past the stratosphere of success as a private company due to his sheer brilliance, yes, but also by dint of his cavalier attitude, flouting rules, regulations, and courtesies along the way. He was the root cause of many of Uber's current woes either directly on his orders or indirectly by his implicit permissiveness. Just look at this roster of other publicized Uber problems that had unfolded or were unfolding parallel to the internal investigations and housecleaning (triggered by the Fowler blog post) in the first half of 2017:

---

[276] Newcomer and Stone, "Fall."

- Departures, forced or otherwise, of key personnel of the self-driving team (the original Advanced Technologies Group)

- Alphabet lawsuit versus Uber for stealing intellectual properties related to the former's research and development on self-driving vehicles

- Investigation launched by the US Justice Department to look into Uber's Greyball program

- Reemergence of Indian rape victim's case because of Alexander's firing and a second lawsuit filed by her against Uber for invading her privacy and defaming her

- Federal Trade Commission's scrutiny into Uber's God View

This was a tornado path of destruction that came about under the watch of Kalanick. Clearly, Travis Kalanick needed to go.

Recalling Lacy's discussions with venture capitalists and their tolerance for asshole CEOs, the burgeoning investor revolt was a landmark event. Finally, somebody had woken up to the reality that it couldn't always be just about the money. Also, there was a little band of "misfit" investors about to flout Silicon Valley's unwritten decree: never go to war against a successful company founder-CEO. After the Steve Jobs fiasco, that is, his firing and rehiring at Apple, it became a "cardinal sin" to do so.[277]

When the planning actually started is unclear, but surely, Mitch Kapor's and Freada Kapor Klein's earlier voices of dissent lay along that timeline. Now, the current players of the operation to oust Kalanick were composed of five of Uber's major investors: Benchmark (one of the company's biggest shareholders, represented by Bill Gurley on the board), First Round Capital, Lowercase Capital, Menlo Ventures, and Fidelity Investments.[278] Together, they owned more than 25 percent of Uber stock and represented about 40 percent of its voting power. All five had banded together to write a letter demanding for Kalanick's resignation and the surrender of his controlling board seats. It was delivered to the CEO, who was in Chicago at that time, interviewing Walter Robb, former co-CEO of Whole Foods for the

[277] *Ibid.*
[278] Mike Isaac, "Uber Founder Travis Kalanick Resigns as CEO," *New York Times*, June 21, 2017, https://www.nytimes.com/2017/06/21/technology/uber-ceo-travis-kalanick.amp.html?.

COO job. The messengers were Matt Cohler and Peter Fenton, partners at Benchmark.[279]

According to anonymous sources cited in a *New York Times* article, the letter was titled, "Moving Uber Forward," and stated in no uncertain terms that the company needed new leadership because of his many "missteps that put the company in legal peril."[280] Kalanick had to get out of the way so it could happen. The messengers gave him just a few hours to think about it before they would go public with the allegations.[281] The grace they were willing to give him was, if he resigned, they would tell everybody that he did so on his own terms.

As of this writing, the full contents of the letter had finally been made public.[282] Written in a firm and official tone, it did not leave Kalanick any wiggle room. It acknowledged that he had truly transformed the concept of transportation forever. "We are deeply grateful for your vision

---

[279] Newcomer and Stone, "Fall."

[280] *Ibid.*

[281] Isaac, "Resigns."

[282] Eric Newcomer and Joel Rosenblatt, "Here's the Uber Investor Letter That Forced Travis Kalanick Out," Bloomberg, January 28, 2019, https://www.bloomberg.com/news/articles/2019-01-28/here-s-the-uber-investor-letter-that-forced-travis-kalanick-out.

and tireless efforts over the last eight years, which have created a company whose technology and workforce have transformed the world's idea of transportation."[283] But from that point, the rest of the letter was simply a recap of all the recent discoveries of scandals and missteps within and outside the company. The letter echoed the recommendations of Holder that Uber needed to change. Towards the end, the investors' letter listed what they hoped would happen. Of course, the first item was the call for Kalanick's resignation.

"First, you need to immediately and permanently resign as CEO and transition this leadership role to capable hands. We strongly believe a change in leadership—coupled with effective Board oversight, governance improvements, and other immediate actions— is necessary for Uber to move forward. We need a trusted, experienced, and energetic new CEO who can help Uber navigate through its many current issues, and achieve its full potential."[284]

Kalanick went on panic mode for the rest of the day, consulting and discussing with board members and investors alike. At one point, Huffington called him and they went over the

---

[283] *Ibid.*

[284] *Ibid.*

letter. It appeared as though the letter would just be the preamble to a potential case of fraud against him if he refused to budge. After all that, drained and enervated as he was already by "five months of pummeling,"[285] Kalanick finally capitulated and resigned as CEO, signing the necessary papers in front of the messengers, who were shocked by his unexpected acquiescence.

In a statement, Kalanick said, "I love Uber more than anything in the world and, at this difficult moment in my personal life, I have accepted the investors' request to step aside, so that Uber can go back to building rather than be distracted with another fight."[286] Gurley took to Twitter to commend Kalanick, tweeting, "There will be many pages in the history books devoted to @travisk — very few entrepreneurs have had such a lasting impact on the world."[287]

However, the twist to this story was that the *New York Times* piece[288] came out about his resignation, which infuriated him. It no longer looked like he had left "on his own terms." Now, it was a Benchmark-organized coup, so he

---

[285] Newcomer and Stone, "Fall."
[286] Isaac, "Resigns."
[287] *Ibid*.
[288] Isaac, "Resigns."

reneged on the surrender of his board seats and started to plot a counter-coup.[289] Benchmark, in response, sued Kalanick for fraud and breach of his fiduciary duties.[290]

Essentially, its lawsuit was based on Kalanick's decision to expand the number of board seats, which the investor argued was invalid because he had withheld material information prior to the vote.[291] A small victory for Kalanick was that the court moved the case to arbitration. Eventually, five months after filing the case, in January 2018, Benchmark dropped it under the condition that Uber was going to sell a sizable stake to SoftBank,[292] a Japanese multinational holding conglomerate based in Tokyo, at a discounted value of $48 billion, down from its most recent valuation of $68 billion. After the deal was completed, it made SoftBank the largest shareholder of Uber, holding 15 percent

---

[289] Newcomer and Stone, "Fall."

[290] *Ibid*.

[291] Dan Primack, "Scoop: Benchmark Capital Sues Travis Kalanick for Fraud," Axios, August 10, 2017, https://www.axios.com/scoop-benchmark-capital-sues-travis-kalanick-for-fraud-1513304764-18c62fe5-c80e-4fec-ad1b-135ffaafa1ec.html.

[292] *Wikipedia*, s.v. "SoftBank Group," accessed March 11, 2019, https://en.wikipedia.org/wiki/SoftBank_Group.

equity.[293]

But how did SoftBank's entry into Uber affect the rest of the shareholding? It diluted everybody's shares, which was the main intent in the first place. Part of the Holder recommendations was about decreasing the power and influence Kalanick wielded within the company. This was now the perfect setup for that to happen. Before Kalanick had left, there were only seven board seats available and most of the board members then were his close allies. With SoftBank on the board, the number of seats went up to 17, effectively decentralizing power. Kalanick still controls three, while SoftBank, two.[294]

(One interesting side note about the SoftBank deal: Emil Michael was hired as a consultant by the Japanese conglomerate to help it navigate the complex deal. For that service alone,

---

[293] Heather Somerville, "SoftBank Is Now Uber's Largest Shareholder as Deal Closes," Reuters, January 18, 2018, https://www.reuters.com/article/us-uber-softbank-tender/softbank-is-now-ubers-largest-shareholder-as-deal-closes-idUSKBN1F72WL.

[294] Rani Molla and Theodore Schleifer, "Here's Who Controls Uber after Its Megadeal with SoftBank," Recode, January 8, 2018, https://www.recode.net/2018/1/8/16865598/uber-softbank-control-board-power-stocks-benchmark-travis-kalanick-dara-khosrowshahi.

Michael took home $4 million.[295] Obviously, this was already after he had resigned from Uber, so there wouldn't have been a conflict of interest.)

Meanwhile, the hunt was on for Kalanick's replacement. Jeffrey Immelt, former CEO of General Electric, was mentioned, but the board suspected he was merely going to serve as a backdoor for Kalanick's eventual return a la Jobs. There was also Expedia CEO Dara Khosrowshahi, who was referred to Kalanick by Uber investor, TPG Capital. Kalanick flew out to Seattle to meet with him there.[296]

Kalanick continued to meddle in Uber affairs. Frankly, telling you about them in detail would be way too tiresome because they appeared to be nothing more than manifestations of a child who simply could not let go of a favorite toy confiscated from him for bad behavior. Daily phone calls to executives. Requests for updates of company operations. An order to the security team to look into an employee's email. The

---

[295] Simon Goodley, "Ex-Uber Boss Was Paid $4 Million by Investor That Acquired 17.5% Stake," *Guardian*, March 31, 2018, https://www.theguardian.com/technology/2018/mar/31/ex-uber-boss-was-paid-4m-by-investor-that-acquired-175-stake.
[296] Newcomer and Stone, "Fall."

interim 16-person committee filling in for a CEO had had enough. The team issued a letter to the board to stop the intrusions. Obviously, it was addressed solely to Kalanick, who still sat on the board and controlled two more seats.[297]

Here, I'll pause for a bit and bring in someone essential whom you might have missed. Someone who was part of the birth of Uber, before the company grew too big for its crib. That someone, of course, is the other half of the founding tandem of Uber, Garrett Camp. While last you heard of him was when I was giving their personal histories, Camp has always been there. On a pragmatic level, he remains a board member, partly responsible for how the company is steered towards achieving its vision, mission, and goals. On a metaphysical level, he is possibly the perfect balance to Kalanick's brash bro persona. Maybe that is why he responded in the way that he did when things fell apart at Uber.

So in the midst of all the chaos of 2017, Camp penned a short piece for *Medium*,[298] in response to everything that was happening at

---

[297] *Ibid*.
[298] Garrett Camp, "Uber's Path Forward," *Medium*, June 20, 2017, https://medium.com/@gc/ubers-path-forward-b59ec9bd4ef6.

the company he created with Kalanick. He recognized that part of the problem was that Uber grew way too fast before they could set proper structures in place to support it. Their focus in the early years was expansion—they had to be in every metropolis worldwide, but they forgot to reinforce the culture within that would prepare them to interact with people in those global metropolises who were so different from themselves. They didn't listen as well as they should have.

But Camp didn't just stop at beating his chest and issuing the essential *mea culpa* cries. He acknowledged that there was hope for all to be had because they were able to identify the attitudes, values, and worldviews that needed to be overhauled. They were now listening and they were ready to act upon what they had heard. He shared an anecdote and the insight it inspired:

"Last week I heard a story that really stuck with me. A college professor made a comment that 'Uber has liberated grandmothers worldwide,' based on the mobility Uber has brought to her mother. And it made me remember that while many mistakes have been made, Uber has changed millions of people's lives for the better, bringing mobility to those who need it most. It's important to remember the positive impact Uber has on the world, and how important our work here is."[299]

He further wrote that they should now hold themselves to a higher standard going forward. He believed that there was still much that Uber could offer the world, but only "once we have additional leadership and training in place, and evolve our culture to be more inclusive and respectful."[300]

At some point, Camp had to quell rumors about a Kalanick comeback as CEO, so he wrote an email to Uber staff, explaining the situation. The board had already narrowed down its choices to just four candidates by then.[301] The key paragraph in Camp's email stated, "Our CEO search is the board's top priority. It's time for a new chapter, and the right leader for our next phase of growth. Despite rumors, I'm sure you've seen in the news, Travis is not returning as CEO. We are committed to hiring a new,

---

[299] *Ibid*.
[300] *Ibid*.
[301] Johana Bhuiyan, "Uber Board Member and Cofounder Garrett Camp Says Travis Kalanick Is Not Coming Back as CEO," Recode, August 7, 2017, https://www.recode.net/2017/8/7/16108778/garrett-camp-uber-travis-kalanick-ceo.

world-class CEO to lead Uber."[302]

If Camp's written sentiments at *Medium* were indicative of what the rest of the board felt, then it was no surprise that, in spite of Kalanick's unwanted and insistent intrusions into Uber's daily affairs, the company still managed to hire a new CEO in Khosrowshahi. He was everything Kalanick "wasn't or couldn't be: humble, a good listener, and a diplomat."[303]

Almost immediately after assuming office, Khosrowshahi's baptism of fire came in the form of a crisis from London. The transport regulator in the British capital refused to renew Uber's license to operate because it simply was not seen as "fit and proper" to be given one.[304] Transport for London emphasized that it held taxis and private hire cars to a high standard primarily because they should be able to keep passenger safety foremost in their operations. Uber had shown itself to be a regular flouter of TfL's regulations. It couldn't even abide by the simplest and most fundamental of those rules,

[302] *Ibid.*

[303] Newcomer and Stone, "Fall."

[304] Natasha Lomas, "Uber Loses Its License to Operate," TechCrunch, September 22, 2017, https://techcrunch.com/2017/09/22/uber-loses-its-license-to-operate-in-london/.

including the ones that governed how medical certificates and background checks were obtained.[305]

Tom Elvidge of Uber in London tried to salvage the situation, of course, by deflecting the issue. He issued an official statement, focusing on the fact that the ban was going to deprive millions of app users and tens of thousands of drivers their rides and livelihoods respectively.[306] He did have a paragraph to address the points the regulator saw were Uber's failings:

"Drivers who use Uber are licensed by Transport for London and have been through the same enhanced Disclosure and Barring Service background checks as black cab drivers. Our pioneering technology has gone further to enhance safety with every trip tracked and recorded by GPS. We have always followed TfL rules on reporting serious incidents and have a dedicated team who work closely with the Metropolitan Police. As we have already told TfL, an independent review has found that 'Greyball' has never been used or considered in the United Kingdom for the purposes cited by

---

[305] *Ibid.*
[306] *Ibid.*

TfL."[307]

Brave words from Elvidge, but they sounded to me more defensive than enlightening, which really didn't make the regulator budge from its position either. Even the mayor of London, Sadiq Khan, supported the TfL's decision. "It would be wrong if TfL continued to license Uber if there is any way that this could pose a threat to Londoners' safety and security."[308] Considering that Uber was already walking on thin ice after its alleged "price gouging" during the London Bridge terror attack, which killed seven people, it was clear that neither the regulator nor the mayor was going to give Uber any wiggle room to negotiate itself out of the ban—even if Uber did make amends by refunding passengers for their rides on that day of terror.[309] And that was the deep end waiting for the new CEO to jump into.

So when London revoked Uber's license to operate that month of September 2017, Khosrowshahi hadn't even warmed his seat yet

---

[307] *Ibid.*

[308] *Ibid.*

[309] "Uber Has Refunded Passengers after London Bridge Terror Attack," BBC, June 5, 2017, http://www.bbc.co.uk/newsbeat/article/40158459/uber-has-refunded-passengers-after-london-bridge-terror-attack.

in San Francisco HQ. He flew out to London to meet with regulators and to figure out a solution. I cannot even begin to imagine what sort of steep learning curve that was for him to catch up on everything while he was airborne. Was he going to be up to scratch or a disappointment?

If there was anything that Khosrowshahi's baptism of fire showed, it was that he was indeed the right candidate for the job. He did step up. It took him roughly a year to get back Uber's license to operate in London, but he managed. In the course of those days of negotiations with TfL, he also published an open letter: "On behalf of everyone at Uber globally, I apologize. We will appeal this decision on behalf of millions of Londoners, but we do so with the knowledge that we must also change."[310] This happened not even one month after Khosrowshahi assumed his new position. He didn't just **sound** like he was in charge. He was **the** man in charge. And that was what set the tone for his now ongoing tenure at Uber. He is in control, but he is also a listening leader.

Supposedly, Kalanick had privately told people that he thought Khosrowshahi's apology tour

---

[310] Newcomer and Stone, "Fall."

was a mistake.[311] Coming from the man who pretty much broke the rules left and right, that was quite understandable. Well, the guy is entitled to his own opinion. Anyway, it probably didn't compute in his brain. And it didn't really matter because he no longer sat as the CEO of Uber. In fact, he had absolutely nothing to do with the hiring of the new COO, Barney Harford. Yes, that all-important position that would have been a full partner to Kalanick's own had Kalanick remained in power.[312]

And so ended the Kalanick era at Uber.

---

[311] *Ibid.*
[312] *Ibid.*

Chapter 7: Life After the Wunderkind Era

Khosrowshahi was an Iranian born to wealth, but there are no records of him ever strutting about with a sense of entitlement. If his professional journey was any indication of how he worked, then he was one who rolled up his sleeves and got busy and dirty in the trenches. Before he joined Uber as the new chief executive officer, post-Kalanick era, he was the CEO of Expedia, one of the largest online travel companies in the world.[313] Under his leadership, "the gross value of its hotel and other travel bookings more than quadrupled and its pre-tax earnings more than doubled."[314] Apparently, Khosrowshahi was not just an expert executive but also a loved leader at the travel company. He was named one of the highest-rated CEOs on Glassdoor,[315] a website

---

[313] "Dara Khosrowshahi," Uber, accessed March 11, 2019, https://www.uber.com/en-KE/newsroom/leadership/dara-khosrowshahi/.
[314] "Uber Picks Dara Khosrowshahi as Its New Boss," *Economist*, September 2, 2017, https://www.economist.com/business/2017/09/02/uber-picks-dara-khosrowshahi-as-its-new-boss.
[315] *Wikipedia*, s.v. "Glassdoor," accessed March 11, 2019, https://en.wikipedia.org/wiki/Glassdoor.

where current and former employees can anonymously rate companies and their management.

The wealth of Khosrowshahi's family did not happen by chance. From all indications, they had a pedigree of entrepreneurship in their blood. "His family founded the Alborz Investment Company, a diversified conglomerate involved in pharmaceuticals, chemicals, food, distribution, packaging, trading, and services."[316] It also appeared that many of his relatives were already in the tech space themselves.[317] His second cousin, Avid Larizadeh Duggan, was a general partner in GV. Another cousin, Amir Khosrowshahi, was chief technology officer of AI products at Intel. Yet another cousin (once removed), Farzad Khosrowshahi, was director of engineering at Google G Suite.[318]

When Khosrowshahi joined Uber in late August 2017, he did not receive a tidily packaged logistics company from Kalanick. You and I had

[316] *Wikipedia*, s.v. "Dara Khosrowshahi," accessed March 11, 2019, https://en.wikipedia.org/wiki/Dara_Khosrowshahi.
[317] Robert Hackett, "Uber's CEO Comes from What May Be the World's Most Techie Family," *Fortune*, November 17, 2017, http://fortune.com/2017/11/17/uber-ceo-dara-khosrowshahi/.
[318] Hackett "Uber's."

already gone through all the sordid details of that chapter in Uber's history. So, we know, in other words, Khosrowshahi was inheriting a huge pile of doo doo from his predecessor. He had a lot of fires to put out inside and outside the organization. However, he wasn't filling in big shoes, that is, he wasn't an incompetent coming into a role ill-suited for him. I'm not discrediting Kalanick at all because he did have huge feet—and therefore huge oxfords to match, but Khosrowshahi also did come with his own pair of gigantic brogues. And boy did he walk in those to match his talk that first year of his tenure as Uber CEO. He led in his own peculiar style.

Fortune published a sort of assessment/commentary of Khosrowshahi's first year as CEO and it was generally positive.[319] It recognized that Khosrowshahi's work was almost impossible, but he was able to pull it off, showing "that moral courage and strategic tradeoffs can drive improved performance. In doing so, he broke past corporate norms and brought reform in three

---

[319] Tim J. Smith, "Uber Is Finally Growing Up," *Fortune*, August 22, 2017, http://fortune.com/2018/08/22/uber-ceo-new-york-london/.

key areas."[320]

The first area that Khosrowshahi changed was that involving Uber's relationship with regulators and regulations. With the suspension of London operations, for instance, he showed that humility can work even in the often rough-and-tumble negotiations between companies and government entities. He seemed to have impressed London's director of licensing enough for the said director to appreciate publicly that Uber was now asking for permission and not forgiveness to resume business.[321] So different from how Kalanick did things in the past.

Apparently, Khosrowshahi's humble approach paid off because, in June 2018, Uber was granted a new license but was put on probation for 15 months. It was decreed to be a "fit and proper" operator after being judged the opposite the previous year.[322] Transport for London, the regulatory agency for the British capital's transportation system, was initially concerned by, among many things, the

---

[320] *Ibid*.

[321] *Ibid*.

[322] "Uber Granted Short-Term License to Operate in London," BBC, June 26, 2018, https://www.bbc.com/news/business-44612837.

ineffectual crime reporting system of the company. Uber was supposed to report any crime involving its drivers directly to the police. Instead, in Uber's old system, reports were being filed with the TfL only. That was now going to change. Uber made a commitment to enact several more improvements to its operations.

Khosrowshahi also reversed Uber's stance and no longer pursued the restoration of UberPOP in Spain and Germany, among other countries that used to have the low-cost ride option. The director of Uber's Southwest Europe operations blogged, "We are changing the way we do business, putting integrity at the core of every decision we make and working hard to earn the trust of the cities in which we operate."[323] Uber was evidently declaring that compliance was going to be the name of its game henceforth. Considering all the run-ins Uber had with regulators previously, this was a step in the right direction to avoid more conflict that it certainly could not afford to have, as it moved towards an IPO.

The second area of improvement in Uber's scorecard involved its relationships with

---

[323] Smith, "Finally."

competitors. For instance, there was that humongous headache of a lawsuit filed by Alphabet against Uber. I had mentioned about it already before, but I want to remind you here that Uber's settlement with Google's parent company came in the form of a .34 percent equity stake. It was a great move by Uber because it reined in any potential bad press and distraction before they could even happen.[324] Khosrowshahi's leadership style seemed to point to an awareness of the future rather than just the here and now. He was mindful that (1) they shouldn't make an enemy of Alphabet because it was a shareholder in Uber via GV. They deserved to be afforded certain courtesies. (2) The sooner they could get the lawsuit out of the picture, the sooner and better they could focus on the essentials of working towards an IPO. What was paramount was the longevity and endurance of Uber.

De-escalation was also at play when Uber retreated from Russia and Southeast Asia. "This kind of strategic decision-making demonstrates that Uber is no longer focused solely on growth and world domination. It may even be finally focused on profits."[325] From an investor's

---

[324] *Ibid*.
[325] *Ibid*.

perspective, money in the bank is without a doubt far more important than hundreds of pins dotting a map.

The third key area of reform under Khosrowshahi involved Uber's housecleaning efforts. After soliciting thorough feedback from Uber employees (two dozen focus groups, 1,200 ideas submitted, 22,000 votes cast and counted), he rewrote the cultural norms of the company with new mantras. "We do the right thing. Period." "We celebrate differences." "We value ideas over hierarchy."[326] No more of the toe-stepping, be hustlin', win-at-all-costs bro cheers to motivate them and to guide their work. Getting ahead of the rest of the logistics industry didn't have to be cutthroat all the time. Sometimes, being a goody-two-shoes could still win.

Khosrowshahi had also purged management. Aside from accepting the resignation of the HR chief accused of systematically dismissing complaints of race-based discrimination,[327] he had allowed several more departures. Of the 16

---

[326] *Ibid.*

[327] Jessi Hempel, "One Year in, the Real Work Begins for Uber's CEO," Wired, September 6, 2018, https://www.wired.com/story/dara-khosrowshahi-uber-ceo-problems-lyft/.

members of Kalanick's management team (you know the one tasked supposedly to run the company while he went on leave), only seven remained. But it's still a work-in-progress for Khosrowshahi concerning increased diversity (read: more women, more minority representation) at Uber.[328] But then again, because this is an endemic situation across a majority of corporations worldwide, it's not like he should be pressured or expected to solve it overnight.

One of the foremost reasons the Holder investigations were made was because of Fowler's blog post, alleging sexual misconduct and harassment. A year later, under Khosrowshahi's leadership, the company came up with a very clear list of actions that would constitute sexual misconduct and sexual assault.

Sexual Misconduct: staring or leering; comments or gestures (asking personal questions); comments or gestures (comments about appearance); comments or gestures (flirting); comments or gestures (explicit gestures); comments or gestures (explicit comments); displaying indecent material;

---

[328] Smith, "Growing."

indecent photography without consent; soliciting sexual content; masturbation/indecent exposure; verbal threat of sexual assault.[329]

Sexual Assault: attempted touching (non-sexual body part); attempted kissing (non-sexual body part); attempted touching (sexual body part); attempted kissing (sexual body part); non-consensual touching (non-sexual body part); non-consensual kissing (non-sexual body part); attempted non-consensual sexual penetration; non-consensual touching: sexual body part; non-consensual kissing: sexual body part; non-consensual sexual penetration.[330]

The creation of this list was especially significant because this was the trigger point for the tailspin of Uber in 2017. The list was everything now, the perfect criteria by which the company could clean up its internal culture. It may not be a coincidence that just a month before this list was publicized, another top executive resigned from Uber after reports of

[329] Alison Griswold, "Uber Has Defined 21 Categories of Sexual Misconduct, from Leering to Rape," Quartz, November 13, 2018, https://qz.com/1460759/uber-defines-21-categories-of-sexual-misconduct-from-leering-to-rape/.
[330] Griswold, "Uber."

sexual misconduct.[331] Cameron Poetzscher was the head of corporate development. He was responsible for some of the biggest deals in the company's history: Grab in Southeast Asia and the entry of SoftBank as an investor.

By all indications, judging from Silicon Valley culture specifically and corporate culture generally, it was unlikely that Poetzscher was going to be the last executive casualty in a sexual misconduct allegation. But against the backdrop of the #metoo movement (after all, Uber does not exist in a vacuum), it was a clear indication that Uber was committed to cleaning house against all costs, even if it meant losing its high performers. No one was going to operate with impunity anymore.

Another moment that possibly enhanced Khosrowshahi's scorecard was a development in Uber's Advanced Technologies Group. First, let me refresh your memory. I had already told you about the Uber-Alphabet settlement with regards to allegedly stolen intellectual properties. I had also narrated to you the self-driving car accident that had killed a pedestrian

[331] Dara Kerr, "Uber's Head Dealmaker Resigns after Reports of Sexual Misconduct," CNET, October 22, 2018, https://www.cnet.com/news/ubers-head-dealmaker-resigns-after-reports-of-sexual-misconduct/.

crossing the street. What I probably hadn't shown you clearly enough was that the settlement happened in February 2018 and then the accident, in March 2018. Seen side by side, the two incidents seemed like the worst possible case of karma for Uber. The months-long suspension of its operations after all that was understandable.

But here was the silver lining in the ATG clouds: in spite of the group's very rough beginnings, Toyota came on board in August 2018 to invest $500 million for a "partnership that will combine Toyota's carmaking expertise with Uber's autonomous tech and ride-hailing platform."[332] The agreement would bring together the two companies to develop self-driving Toyota Sienna minivans ready for deployment in Uber's network by 2021.[333]

While Khosrowshahi appeared to be doing a (mostly) splendid job in the very areas where Kalanick and his team used to fail, it was inadvertent that he couldn't win 'em all, especially when the issues were part of his inheritance from Kalanick. For instance, Uber was finally meted a fine by British and Dutch authorities in the combined amount of $1.17

[332] Hempel, "One."
[333] *Ibid*.

million for the data breach orchestrated by hackers. That incident exposed the personal information of millions of drivers and riders to the criminals. Uber had paid $100,000 to the latter to keep them quiet and to convince them to delete all the data they had collected. The misdeed happened in 2016 and even top Uber executives knew about it at the time it happened, but it was never revealed to the public until after a year later.[334] In the US, Uber's penalty came in the form of a payout of $148 million to settle any claims.[335]

Another bit of setback for Uber involved, as usual, its drivers. Across the many cities in which Uber operated and all throughout 2018, strikes were called to protest the unfair and minimal earnings drivers collected from the company. In Kenya, the UK, India, Spain, South Africa, and a few other countries, drivers went offline and did not respond to any ride requests. In Great Britain, riders were specifically

[334] Elizabeth Schulze, "Uber Fined nearly $1.2 Million by British and Dutch Authorities for 2016 Data Breach," CNBC, November 27, 2018, https://www.cnbc.com/2018/11/27/uber-fined-more-than-1-million-dollars-by-uk-and-dutch-authorities.html.
[335] *Ibid*.

requested not to cross the digital picket line.[336]

Then, in perhaps one of the hardest blows to Uber and its drivers, the city council of New York passed several bills in August 2018 to control the ride-hailing industry. The regulations set a cap to the number of drivers who can work for Uber and Lyft in a year, but it also established minimum pay rates for the drivers. Lastly, they also required the companies to report each trip details: duration, costs, driver's earnings, and the company's commission.[337] With New York being Uber's largest market, the new city council rules may very well set a precedent across the globe that will definitely affect Uber's bottom line. And not very likely in a good way. As of this writing, it was still unclear exactly how many more cities were going to adopt measures similar to those in New York.

However, it couldn't be denied that Khosrowshahi's leadership was making a

[336] Ben Quinn, "Uber UK Strike: Users Urged Not to Cross 'Digital Picket Line,'" *Guardian*, October 9, 2018, https://www.theguardian.com/technology/2018/oct/09/uber-uk-strike-users-urged-not-to-cross-digital-picket-line.

[337] Alexia Fernández Campbell, "New York City Cracks Down on Uber and Other Ride-Hailing Apps," Vox, August 9, 2018, https://www.vox.com/2018/8/8/17664424/new-york-uber-taxis-driver-law.

difference in the company. Uber continued with its company-wide overhaul of cultures, systems, and goals, its advance towards an IPO did not show any signs of slowing down. As of this writing, it looks set to happen in April 2019, just a little after Lyft's own IPO, which debuts at the end of March 2019.[338]

At this point, the Uber IPO may become one of the top five biggest listings in history on the New York Stock Exchange.[339] To date, the valuation of Uber still hovers in the neighborhood of $120 billion. In order to qualify for a top-five slot, it only needs to float 16% of its shares.[340] Uber is doing its IPO differently from Lyft's. While the latter is choosing to trade with Nasdaq, the usual choice for tech IPOs before, Uber is going with NYSE where Alibaba, Snap, and Twitter went. How it will fare there is anybody's guess, but trading in the place where other giants go to trade is not

---

[338] Carl O'Donnell and Heather Somerville, "Exclusive: Uber Plans to Kick Off IPO in April—Sources," Reuters, March 14, 2019, https://www.reuters.com/article/us-uber-ipo-exclusive/exclusive-uber-plans-to-kick-off-ipo-in-april-sources-idUSKCN1QV2QU.

[339] Eric Newcomer and Bloomberg, "Uber IPO Could Be One of Five Biggest NYSE Listings in History," *Fortune*, March 21, 2019, http://fortune.com/2019/03/21/uber-ipo-nyse-listing-lyft-nasdaq/.

[340] *Ibid*.

such a bad way to go at all.

Meantime, Kalanick is still very much alive and well. Although he went quiet for several months following his resignation as Uber CEO and appeared only oh so briefly in court to testify for the Uber-Alphabet case, he reemerged to announce the launch of his new private equity fund called 10100, in early March 2018. Very likely named after the address of his childhood home, 10100 will have "large-scale job creation" as its primary mission.[341] The fund was to be applied to for-profit investments in "real estate, e-commerce, and 'emerging innovation' in China and India, as well as nonprofit work focusing on education and 'the future of cities.'"[342] Kalanick's new venture appeared to be closely related to a lot of work that he had already been doing in the first place, that is, helping to start and to grow fledgling businesses.[343]

[341] Julia Carrie Wong, "Ex-Uber CEO Travis Kalanick Reveals New Project: a 'Job Creation' Fund," *Guardian*, March 8, 2018,
https://www.theguardian.com/business/2018/mar/07/uber-ceo-travis-kalanick-10100-investment-fund.
[342] *Ibid*.
[343] Jonathan Shieber, "Travis Kalanick Is Launching a Venture Fund," TechCrunch, March 7, 2018,

Fresh from the SoftBank deal, Kalanick was likely swimming in tons of actual banked cash to make this equity fund a reality for himself. According to a rough estimate, he should have received $1.4 billion for his 29-percent stake.[344]

About two weeks after his fund launch, on March 20, 2018, Kalanick tweeted that he had acquired a controlling interest in City Storage Systems, which he described as "a holding company focused on the redevelopment of distressed real estate assets particularly in the areas of parking, retail, and industrial."[345] To further clarify exactly what the company did, its website explained, "We provide infrastructure and software that enables food operators to open delivery-only locations with minimal capital expenditure and time."[346] Another way of putting it would be to say that CSS "wants to redevelop industrial real estate to cater to a

---

https://techcrunch.com/2018/03/07/travis-kalanick-is-launching-a-venture-fund/.

[344] *Ibid*.

[345] Johana Bhuiyan and Theodore Schleifer, "Travis Kalanick Is Buying a New Company That Rehabs Real Estate and Will Run It as CEO," Recode, March 20, 2018, https://www.recode.net/2018/3/20/17145032/travis-kalanick-uber-new-job-ceo-real-estate-startup-city-storage-systems.

[346] *Ibid*.

future based around the Internet."[347]

According to Kalanick, there is "$10 trillion in these real estate assets that will need to be repurposed for the digital era in the coming years," based on in-house analysis on global parking and retail assets.[348] Previously called CloudKitchens, CSS was led by Diego Berdakin, an entrepreneur based in Los Angeles and an early Uber investor. Kalanick's entry into the startup with $150 million bought out outside investors.[349]

As always with Kalanick, you deal in big numbers and big dreams, once he gets started and puts on his CEO cap. You do have to give it to the wunderkind. It's not like he hadn't set a track record of success. Just look at Uber now.

Apparently, Uber is now busy with its own kitchens dedicated to its food delivery app, Uber Eats.[350] It has leased real estate in Paris to

---

[347] Dennis Lynch, "Pizza Will Be Served: Inside Travis Kalanick's Real Estate Revolution," Real Deal, May 7, 2018, https://therealdeal.com/la/2018/05/07/pizza-will-be-served-inside-travis-kalanicks-real-estate-revolution/.
[348] Lynch, "Pizza."
[349] Bhuiyan and Schleifer, "Travis."
[350] Olivia Feld, "Uber to Open 'Dark Kitchens' to Expand Food Delivery Business," Telegraph, March 11, 2019, https://www.telegraph.co.uk/technology/2019/03/11/uber-open-dark-kitchens-expand-food-delivery-business/.

accommodate the facilities, which are supposed to be fully stocked with ovens, fridges, sinks, stoves[351]—all the equipment necessary to make food deliveries possible. Sound familiar? It appears as though Uber is overlapping with Kalanick's plans, setting both up to go head-to-head in the food delivery space.[352] While Uber had chosen the City of Lights as its test site, Kalanick has been casting about in the Chinese market for his, as usual, aggressive plans for global expansion.[353] It would be such a tasty victory for him, if he achieved a foothold right where he suffered one of his biggest losses as Uber CEO.

It is actually not a surprise that there's an imminent war about to happen in so many aspects of the food industry. Right from production to preparation all the way to delivery. Silicon Valley has been immersed in it

---

[351] *Ibid.*

[352] Eric Newcomer, "Uber and Travis Kalanick Are in Business Again. This Time, as Competitors," Bloomberg, March 11, 2019, https://www.bloomberg.com/news/articles/2019-03-11/uber-and-travis-kalanick-are-in-business-again-this-time-as-competitors.

[353] Nicole Jao, "Briefing: Former Uber CEO Travis Kalanick Looks to China for Kitchen-Sharing Business," Technode, February 1, 2019, https://technode.com/2019/02/01/briefing-former-uber-ceo-travis-kalanick-to-bring-shared-kitchen-to-china/.

for some time now with its intermittent fasting, biohacking, and similar "trends." But more than viewing them as trends—and therefore temporal, until the newest one comes up—all these efforts are actually directed towards addressing issues of one of the most basic human needs: food. People need it fast. People need more of it. People need it to be more accessible and so on and so forth. So when Uber and Kalanick's CSS—or CloudKitchens really sounds more appropriate—introduce innovations, it's because food concerns are fast becoming a priority to humans. They are literally a matter of life or death. Of course, both Uber and Kalanick want to be first to market in providing solutions. For Uber especially, it is essential for the kitchens, and therefore Uber Eats, to succeed. Combined, they could create as much profit as the ride-hailing app itself. Or even surpass it. Nothing could be better for the company when it's heading towards its IPO. So Uber is doing its food business innovation in Paris, while Kalanick is making his global first step in China. Will Kalanick be able to pull off another Uber-sized triumph?

And speaking about global expansion, Kalanick wasn't just busy with cooking up his digital-age kitchens, he was also investing in other industries. In March 2019, news came out that an Indonesian startup received a seed fund of $7.6 million from various investors, including Kalanick. Kargo is set to be an "Uber for trucks" and was co-founded by a former Uber executive, Tiger Fang, who managed Uber's business in Chengdu, among many other assignments.[354] The Kargo investment represented Kalanick's first official foray into the Southeast Asian market.

As for Camp, Kalanick's once partner-in-crime, I had already mentioned his first company's, StumbleUpon, shutdown in 2018, after more than 15 years of operations, in order to give way to a new discovery platform, Mix. Mix itself was born from another Camp business, Expa, which was essentially a special sort of business incubator because it benefitted from Camp's distilled experiences with StumbleUpon and Uber. He had also committed to donating half his wealth to charity through the Giving Pledge, a global campaign to encourage the richest people in the world to give most of their assets to philanthropy, which Bill and Melissa Gates started in 2010.

---

[354] Jon Russell, "Indonesia's Kargo Comes Out of Stealth with $7.6 Million from Travis Kalanick, Sequoia, and Others," TechCrunch, March 22, 2019, https://techcrunch.com/2019/03/22/kargo/.

In early 2018, there was talk about Camp creating a new cryptocurrency,[355] but to-date, nothing concrete had materialized since that announcement. In other words, Uber's other co-founder continues to steer clear of the public eye.

An Uberized World

These days, when I think about smartphones, I find it hard to imagine how I managed to live my early years without them. The utilities they provide are almost limitless: dictionary, movie screen, book, calendar, voice recorder, camera, game console, file organizer, word processor . . . trust me when I say that, truly, the list is endless. My personal history has a pre- and post-smartphone mile marker. And that's the same experience I have with Uber. I had a different life before Uber and after I started using it. They are distinct.

My first Uber ride was with friends. We were visiting New York at that time and staying at an Airbnb brownstone in Brooklyn. We wanted to go to Manhattan on a bone-chilling, sleety late

---

[355] Fitz Tepper, "Uber Cofounder Garret Camp Is Creating a New Cryptocurrency," TechCrunch, March 1, 2018, https://techcrunch.com/2018/03/01/uber-co-founder-garrett-camp-is-creating-a-new-cryptocurrency/.

January night to hang out at a bar highly recommended on Yelp. We were not going to be deterred by some silly polar vortex swirling about us. So, my friend requested an Uber. It arrived within minutes and that felt so magical. It was not my first time in New York, so I knew that without Uber, my friends and I would have had to stomp our way to the nearest subway station to get to where we needed to go. Forget about hailing a cab. It was a snowy Friday night. In Brooklyn. Fat chance of that going down easy. But there we were. In an Uber. Hassle-free. It felt so wonderful to be in the warm comforts of a beautiful, leather-interior town car.

I'm telling you this personal experience as I wrap up the story of Uber because, as horrible as its recent years had been with revelations of sexual misconduct, almost-criminal activities, and careless regard for government rules and regulations, it had introduced the whole world to a different way of getting a ride. Or food. Or work.

Uber's impact is deep and far-reaching. For instance, while the gig economy is not new, Uber contributed to making it a viable possibility for earning a living. Switch on the app, you can start getting customers. Switch it off, you can head out and run errands. Switch it back on to work again when you're ready.

For the most part, drivers' earnings are never quite enough to feed a family of, maybe, four. Just ask the drivers themselves and why you find them calling for a strike every so often. There is a need for reform, so they can get a more decent wage to feed themselves and their loved ones. With the New York City Council's regulations, that situation can certainly change, if other cities adopt them. But I do know a few people who are just thankful that they can drive with Uber at all. It's extra cash for them. Or it's all that they have going for them because life happened. Regardless of how you look at the scenario, the fundamental truth is that Uber had changed the economy, for good or ill.

Uber had, of course, changed the transportation industry forever. On demand. Now that is a very precious phrase nowadays. This society is used to pushing buttons, tapping screens, and swiping right to get what it wants. When it wants. Uber couldn't have been born at any other time than this time because that's what it gives people. Expedited convenience at your fingertips. No more frustrations at being ignored by an empty cab. No more huffing and puffing down the stairs of the subway station only to miss the train by seconds when you're in emergency mode. And if Uber does perfect self-driving vehicles and various forms of air transport, then what could it not do to help you move as effortlessly as possible from point A to point B? Uber submarines? I wouldn't be surprised if that happened in the next few years.

Various countries and cultures have always had food delivery systems in place. In a friend's childhood neighborhood, they knew to expect rice delicacies brought to them for breakfast. Then home-cooked vegetable and meat dishes for lunch. Then afternoon snacks of spring rolls and fried bananas. And, for the evening fare, there was boiled duck's eggs, supposedly an aphrodisiac for the night's shenanigans. All brought right to her family's doorstep. Usually delivered by an elderly with a basket covered by banana leaves.

Uber Eats leveled up that tradition. It can fulfill even your craziest cravings. Just ask any pregnant woman what that sort of accessibility does for her. It's mind-blowing that you're no longer confined to choosing from just the sometimes sad menu of fast food. Or the usual greasy fare from you-know-which restaurants. Now, even restaurants that didn't use to have delivery systems can send over the food you want because there's a mobile app that can facilitate it for you.

Uberization and uberize have now become legitimate words in the English language because the type of service they represent was institutionalized by Uber itself. I'm not saying that Uber invented it. I'm saying that it solidified the concept and made it widespread. From this generation onwards, people will expect nothing less than what it had standardized.

So what more can we expect from Uber in the future? It's anybody's guess, really. Its first decade was characterized by the crazy, unbounded entrepreneurial genius of Kalanick. Khosrowshahi is still too fresh an Uber CEO, as of this writing, to give a clear indication of what his time will look like. But for sure, it will still be great. Because slowly but surely, Uber is becoming its own entity and identity apart from its leaders. It's becoming a tradition, the minimum expectation, inviting the next Uber of the next generation to disrupt it.

Bibliography

Alba, Davey. "Judge Rejects Uber's $100 Million Settlement with Drivers." Wired, August 8, 2016. https://www.wired.com/2016/08/uber-settlement-rejected/.

---. "Some Drivers Really Aren't Happy about the $100 Million Uber Settlement." Wired, May 16, 2016. https://www.wired.com/2016/05/drivers-really-arent-happy-100m-uber-settlement/.

Alfaro, Lyanne. "Uber's CEO Used to Host Intimate Jam Sessions at His Home So Entrepreneurs Could Hash Out Business Ideas." Business Insider, September 8, 2015. https://www.businessinsider.com/uber-ceo-hosted-jam-sessions-at-his-home-for-entrepreneurs-to-hash-out-business-ideas-2015-9?IR=T.

Associated Press in San Francisco. "Uber to Pay $20M over Claims It Misled Drivers over How Much They Would Earn." *Guardian*, January 20, 2017. https://www.theguardian.com/technology/2017/jan/19/uber-settlement-ftc-driver-earnings-car-leases.

Bacharach, Elizabeth. "Uber Has a 'God View' Tool and Was Allegedly Using It to Spy on Celebs." *Cosmopolitan*, December 14, 2016. https://www.cosmopolitan.com/lifestyle/a849 5499/uber-using-god-view-tool-to-spy-on-celebs/.

Balakrishnan, Anita, Jillian D'Onfro, Deirdre Bosa, and Paayal Zaveri. "Uber Settles Dispute with Alphabet's Self-driving Car Unit." CNBC, February 9, 2018. https://www.cnbc.com/2018/02/09/uber-waymo-lawsuit-settlement.html.

BBC. "Trump's Executive Order: Who Does Travel Ban Affect?" February 10, 2017, https://www.bbc.com/news/world-us-canada-38781302.

---. "Uber Granted Short-Term License to Operate in London." BBC, June 26, 2018. https://www.bbc.com/news/business-44612837.

---. "Uber Has Refunded Passengers after London Bridge Terror Attack." BBC, June 5, 2017. http://www.bbc.co.uk/newsbeat/article/40158 459/uber-has-refunded-passengers-after-london-bridge-terror-attack.

---. "Uber Settles Defamation Lawsuit Filed by Indian Rape Victim." December 9, 2017. https://www.bbc.com/news/world-us-canada-42291495.

Bellman, Eric, and Dhanya Ann Thoppil. "How Did Uber Go from Nowhere to Everywhere in India?" *Wall Street Journal*, December 10, 2014. https://blogs.wsj.com/indiarealtime/2014/12/10/how-did-uber-go-from-nowhere-to-everywhere-in-india/.

Berboucha, Meriame. "Uber Self-Driving Car Crash: What Really Happened?" *Forbes*, May 28, 2018. https://www.forbes.com/sites/meriameberbo ucha/2018/05/28/uber-self-driving-car-crash-what-really-happened/#3a6cf67c4dc4.

Bhuiyan, Johana. "Everything You Need to Know about Uber's Turbulent 2017." Recode, August 20, 2017. https://www.recode.net/2017/8/20/16164176/uber-2017-timeline-scandal.

---. "Uber Board Member and Cofounder Garrett Camp Says Travis Kalanick Is Not Coming Back as CEO." Recode, August 7, 2017. https://www.recode.net/2017/8/7/16108778/garrett-camp-uber-travis-kalanick-ceo.

---. "Uber's Head of Finance Has Left the Company." Recode, May 31, 2017. https://www.recode.net/2017/5/31/15722452/uber-finance-gautam-gupta-departure.

---. "Uber's SVP of Business Emil Michael Has Left the Company." Recode, June 12, 2017. https://www.recode.net/2017/6/12/15783204/uber-emil-michael-step-down-resign.

---. "Why the Uber Drivers' Lawyer Settled Their Fight to Become Employees." Recode, April 30, 2016. https://www.recode.net/2016/4/30/11586570/uber-drivers-employees-contractors-lawyer.

---, and Theodore Schleifer. "Travis Kalanick Is Buying a New Company That Rehabs Real Estate and Will Run It as CEO." Recode, March 20, 2018. https://www.recode.net/2018/3/20/17145032/travis-kalanick-uber-new-job-ceo-real-estate-startup-city-storage-systems.

Biddle, Sam. "Uber's Dirty Trick Campaign against NYC Competition Came from the Top." Valleywag, January 24, 2014. http://valleywag.gawker.com/ubers-dirty-trick-campaign-against-nyc-competition-cam-1508280668.

Bosa, Deirdre. "Uber Releases Its First Diversity Report—and It Looks Like Pretty Much Every Other Tech Company." CNBC, March 28, 2017. https://www.cnbc.com/2017/03/28/uber-diversity-report-released.html.

Camp, Garrett. "How I Came Up with Uber – The Startup Mentality with Garrett Camp – Zeitgeist 2016." Interview. Zeitgeist Minds, September 23, 2016. YouTube video, 12:48. https://www.youtube.com/watch?v=_vxk4Z1u7RE.

---. "SU Is Moving to Mix." Medium, May 23, 2018. https://medium.com/@gc/su-is-moving-to-mix-c2c3bff037a5.

---. "Uber's Path Forward." *Medium*, June 20, 2017. https://medium.com/@gc/ubers-path-forward-b59ec9bd4ef6.

Campbell, Alexia Fernández. "New York City Cracks Down on Uber and Other Ride-Hailing Apps." Vox, August 9, 2018. https://www.vox.com/2018/8/8/17664424/new-york-uber-taxis-driver-law.

Carr, Paul Bradley. "'We Call That Boob-er:' The Four Most Awful Things Travis Kalanick Said in His GQ Profile." Pando, February 27,

2014. https://pando.com/2014/02/27/we-call-that-boob-er-the-four-most-awful-things-travis-kalanick-said-in-his-gq-profile/.

Carson, Biz. "Uber Cofounder Garrett Camp Is Back to an Old Problem: Finding Interesting Things on the Internet." *Forbes*, August 1, 2018. https://www.forbes.com/sites/bizcarson/2018/08/01/uber-cofounder-garrett-camp-is-back-to-an-old-problem-finding-interesting-things-on-the-internet/#3e8e58a26c9d.

---. "Uber's Secret Gold Mine: How Uber Eats Is Turning into a Billion-Dollar Business to Rival Grubhub." *Forbes*, February 6, 2019. https://www.forbes.com/sites/bizcarson/2019/02/06/ubers-secret-gold-mine-how-uber-eats-is-turning-into-a-billion-dollar-business-to-rival-grubhub/#6098e4421fa9.

---. "Uber Settles Investigation into 'God View' Tool.'" Business Insider, January 6, 2016. https://www.businessinsider.com/uber-settles-investigation-into-god-view-tool-2016-1?IR=T.

Cave, Damien. "Why Scour Is Not the New Napster." Salon, August 22, 2000. https://www.salon.com/2000/08/22/scour/.

Chen, James. "Unicorn." Investopedia, December 21, 2017. https://www.investopedia.com/terms/u/unicorn.asp.

Chrysanthos, Natassia. "Coles Quietly Expands Uber Eats Trial to Deliver Supermarket Essentials." *Sydney Morning Herald*, March 21, 2019. https://www.smh.com.au/business/companies/coles-quietly-expands-ubereats-trial-to-deliver-supermarket-essentials-20190319-p515k9.html.

CIA World Factbook. "Central America: Puerto Rico." Accessed March 11, 2019. https://www.cia.gov/library/publications/resources/the-world-factbook/geos/rq.html.

Cresci, Elena. "#DeleteUber: How Social Media Turned on Uber." *Guardian*, January 30, 2017. https://www.theguardian.com/technology/2017/jan/30/deleteuber-how-social-media-turned-on-uber.

Crook, Jordan. "Garrett Camp's Latest Expa Project, Mix, Aims to Curate the Web." TechCrunch, accessed March 11, 2019. https://techcrunch.com/2017/08/01/garrett-camps-latest-expa-project-mix-aims-to-curate-the-web/.

Crunchbase. "Uber Funding Rounds."
Accessed March 11, 2019.
https://www.crunchbase.com/organization/ub
er/funding_rounds/funding_rounds_list.

Dallett, Lydia. "This One Stat Shows Just How
Far behind Silicon Valley Is on Gender
Equality." Business Insider, February 4, 2014.
https://www.businessinsider.com/silicon-
valley-and-gender-equality-twitter-2014-
2?IR=T.

DashBurst. "What Is StumbleUpon and How
Does It Work?" Small Business Trends,
updated February 9, 2019.
https://smallbiztrends.com/2014/08/what-is-
stumbleupon-how-do-i-use-it.html.

Dickey, Megan Rose. "Uber Agrees to Pay
Drivers $20 Million to Settle Independent
Contractor." TechCrunch, March 12, 2019.
https://techcrunch.com/2019/03/12/uber-
agrees-to-pay-drivers-20-million-to-settle-
independent-contractor-lawsuit/.

---. "Uber Is Developing an On-demand
Staffing Business." TechCrunch, accessed
March 11, 2019.
https://techcrunch.com/2018/10/18/uber-is-

developing-an-on-demand-staffing-business/.

Economist. "Uber Picks Dara Khosrowshahi as Its New Boss." September 2, 2017. https://www.economist.com/business/2017/09/02/uber-picks-dara-khosrowshahi-as-its-new-boss.

Efrati, Amir. "Uber Group's Visit to Seoul Escort Bar Sparked HR Complaint," Information, March 24, 2017, https://www.theinformation.com/articles/uber-groups-visit-to-seoul-escort-bar-sparked-hr-complaint

Expa. "About." Accessed March 11, 2019. https://www.expa.com/#about.

Feiner, Lauren. "Grubhub Sinks as Analysts Say It's Struggling to Keep Pace with Uber Eats and DoorDash." CNBC, March 19, 2019. https://www.cnbc.com/2019/03/19/grubhub-sinks-as-it-loses-share-to-ubereats-and-doordash.html.

Feld, Olivia. "Uber to Open 'Dark Kitchens' to Expand Food Delivery Business." *Telegraph*, March 11, 2019. https://www.telegraph.co.uk/technology/2019/03/11/uber-open-dark-kitchens-expand-food-delivery-business/.

Fieldstadt, Elisha. "Michigan Uber Driver Jason Dalton Pleads Guilty in Kalamazoo Shooting Spree That Killed 6." NBC, January 7, 2019. https://www.nbcnews.com/news/us-news/michigan-uber-driver-jason-dalton-pleads-guilty-kalamazoo-shooting-spree-n955716.

Fowler, Susan. "Reflecting on One Very, Very Strange Year at Uber." *Susan J. Fowler* (blog), February 19, 2017. https://www.susanjfowler.com/blog/2017/2/19/reflecting-on-one-very-strange-year-at-uber.

Freund, Shlomo. "A Short History of Uber in China: Was It a Failure?" *Forbes*, August 15, 2016. https://www.forbes.com/sites/shlomofreund/2016/08/15/a-short-history-of-uber-in-china-was-it-a-failure/#630e8a673386.

Frommer, Dan. "eBay Dumps StumbleUpon." Business Insider, April 13, 2009. https://www.businessinsider.com/ebay-lets-go-of-stumbleupon-2009-4?IR=T.

Ghoshal, Abhimanyu. "Uber's Southeast Asia Operations Acquired by Grab." Next Web, accessed March 11, 2019. https://thenextweb.com/asia/2018/03/26/ubers-southeast-asia-operations-acquired-by-grab/.

Graser, Marc. "Ovitz Adds Scour to Online Portfolio." *Variety*, June 11, 1999. https://variety.com/1999/digital/news/ovitz-adds-scour-to-online-portfolio-1117502994/.

Griswold, Alison. "Uber Has Defined 21 Categories of Sexual Misconduct, from Leering to Rape," Quartz, November 13, 2018, https://qz.com/1460759/uber-defines-21-categories-of-sexual-misconduct-from-leering-to-rape/.

Goodley, Simon. "Ex-Uber Boss Was Paid $4 Million by Investor That Acquired 17.5% Stake." *Guardian*, March 31, 2018. https://www.theguardian.com/technology/2018/mar/31/ex-uber-boss-was-paid-4m-by-investor-that-acquired-175-stake.

Guardian. "Uber Boss Travis Kalanick's Mother Dies in Boating Accident." May 28, 2017. https://www.theguardian.com/technology/2017/may/28/uber-boss-travis-kalanicks-mother-dies-in-boating-accident.

Hackett, Robert. "Uber's CEO Comes from What May Be the World's Most Techie Family," *Fortune*, November 17, 2017, http://fortune.com/2017/11/17/uber-ceo-dara-khosrowshahi/.

Hartmans, Avery, and Nathan McAlone. "The Story of How Travis Kalanick Built Uber into the Most Feared and Valuable Startup in the World." Business Insider, August 1, 2016. https://www.businessinsider.com/ubers-history?IR=T.

Hatch, Patrick. "Why Woolies Boss Thinks Uber Eats Is a Bigger Threat Than Amazon." *Sunday Morning Herald*, February 24, 2018. https://www.smh.com.au/business/companies/why-woolies-boss-thinks-uber-eats-is-a-bigger-threat-than-amazon-20180223-p4z1gp.html.

Hawkins, Andrew J. "Uber Narrows Its Search for International City to Host 'Flying Taxis.'" Verge, August 30, 2018. https://www.theverge.com/2018/8/30/17795588/uber-elevate-flying-car-international-city-search-drone.

---. "Uber Scores a Big Win in Legal Fight to Keep Drivers as Independent Contractors." Verge, September 25, 2018. https://www.theverge.com/2018/9/25/17901284/uber-drivers-independent-contractors-vs-employees-legal-fight.

Hempel, Jessi. "One Year in, the Real Work Begins for Uber's CEO." Wired, September 6, 2018. https://www.wired.com/story/dara-khosrowshahi-uber-ceo-problems-lyft/.

Hern, Alex. "Uber Employees Spied on Ex-partners, Politicians, and Beyoncé." *Guardian*, December 13, 2016. https://www.theguardian.com/technology/2016/dec/13/uber-employees-spying-ex-partners-politicians-beyonce.

---. "Uber Executive Apologizes after Suggesting the Firm Dig Dirt on Hostile Journalists." *Guardian*, November 18, 2019. https://www.theguardian.com/technology/2014/nov/18/uber-exec-apologises-emil-michael-journalist-sarah-lacy.

---. "Uber Execs Including Travis Kalanick Went to Escort/Karaoke Bar," *Guardian*, March 27, 2017, https://www.theguardian.com/technology/2017/mar/27/uber-execs-including-travis-kalanick-went-to-escortkaraoke-bar.

Heyman, Stephen. "Paris Raises Its Silhouette, but Slowly and Not Easily." *New York Times*, June 3, 2015. https://www.nytimes.com/2015/06/04/arts/international/paris-raises-its-silhouette-but-slowly-and-not-easily.html.

History. "Mankind's Greatest Inventions."
Accessed March 11, 2019.
https://www.history.co.uk/shows/mankind-
the-story-of-all-of-us/articles/mankinds-
greatest-inventions.

Huet, Ellen. "Juries to Decide Landmark Cases
against Uber and Lyft." *Forbes*, March 11,
2015.
https://www.forbes.com/sites/ellenhuet/2015
/03/11/lyft-uber-employee-jury-trial-
ruling/#65707b3964b9.

International Monetary Fund. "Report for
Selected Countries and Subjects." Accessed
March 11, 2019.
https://www.imf.org/external/pubs/ft/weo/2
018/01/weodata/weorept.aspx?pr.x=46&pr.y=
12&sy=2018&ey=2018&scsm=1&ssd=1&sort=c
ountry&ds=.&br=1&c=512%2C946%2C914%2
C137%2C612%2C546%2C614%2C962%2C311
%2C674%2C213%2C676%2C911%2C548%2C1
93%2C556%2C122%2C678%2C912%2C181%2
C313%2C867%2C419%2C682%2C513%2C684
%2C316%2C273%2C913%2C868%2C124%2C9
21%2C339%2C948%2C638%2C943%2C514%2
C686%2C218%2C688%2C963%2C518%2C616
%2C728%2C223%2C836%2C516%2C558%2C

918%2C138%2C748%2C196%2C618%2C278%
2C624%2C692%2C522%2C694%2C622%2C14
2%2C156%2C449%2C626%2C564%2C628%2
C565%2C228%2C283%2C924%2C853%2C233
%2C288%2C632%2C293%2C636%2C566%2C
634%2C964%2C238%2C182%2C662%2C359
%2C960%2C453%2C423%2C968%2C935%2C
922%2C128%2C714%2C611%2C862%2C321%
2C135%2C243%2C716%2C248%2C456%2C46
9%2C722%2C253%2C942%2C642%2C718%2C
643%2C724%2C939%2C576%2C644%2C936%
2C819%2C961%2C172%2C813%2C132%2C726
%2C646%2C199%2C648%2C733%2C915%2C1
84%2C134%2C524%2C652%2C361%2C174%2
C362%2C328%2C364%2C258%2C732%2C656
%2C366%2C654%2C734%2C336%2C144%2C2
63%2C146%2C268%2C463%2C532%2C528%2
C944%2C923%2C176%2C738%2C534%2C578
%2C536%2C537%2C429%2C742%2C433%2C
866%2C178%2C369%2C436%2C744%2C136%
2C186%2C343%2C925%2C158%2C869%2C43
9%2C746%2C916%2C926%2C664%2C466%2
C826%2C112%2C542%2C111%2C967%2C298
%2C443%2C927%2C917%2C846%2C544%2C2
99%2C941%2C582%2C446%2C474%2C666%2
C754%2C668%2C698%2C672&s=PPPGDP&gr
p=0&a=.

Isaac, Mike. "How Uber Deceives the
Authorities Worldwide." *New York Times*,

March 3, 2017.
https://www.nytimes.com/2017/03/03/techn
ology/uber-greyball-program-evade-
authorities.html.

---. "Inside Uber's Aggressive, Unrestrained
Workplace Culture." *New York Times*,
February 22, 2017.
https://www.nytimes.com/2017/02/22/techn
ology/uber-workplace-culture.html?smid=tw-
share&_r=0.

---. "Uber Fires 20 Amid Investigation into
Workplace Culture." *New York Times*, June 6,
2017.
https://www.nytimes.com/2017/06/06/techn
ology/uber-fired.html.

---. "Uber Founder Travis Kalanick Resigns as
CEO." *New York Times*, June 21, 2017.
https://www.nytimes.com/2017/06/21/techno
logy/uber-ceo-travis-kalanick.amp.html?.

Jiayi, Liu. "Uber Officially Enters China with
Shanghai Launch." ZDNet, February 14, 2014.
https://www.zdnet.com/article/uber-officially-
enters-china-with-shanghai-launch/.

Jao, Nicole. "Briefing: Former Uber CEO
Travis Kalanick Looks to China for Kitchen-
Sharing Business." Technode, February 1,

2019. https://technode.com/2019/02/01/briefing-former-uber-ceo-travis-kalanick-to-bring-shared-kitchen-to-china/.

Kalanick, Travis. "Travis Kalanick at Startup School 2012." October 25, 2013, at Y Combinator Startup School on October 20, 2012 in Stanford Memorial Auditorium, produced by Y Combinator and the Stanford Technology Ventures Program. YouTube video, 28:49. https://www.youtube.com/watch?v=rQ6G0Y2_Ujw&t=252s.

---. "Travis Kalanick Interview." Interview. The Late Show with Stephen Colbert, September 11, 2015. YouTube video, 5:54. https://www.youtube.com/watch?v=wGdjLv8neBs.

---. "Travis Kalanick of Uber – TWiST #180." Interview by Jason Calacanis. This Week in Startups, August 16 2011. YouTube video, 1:21:38. https://www.youtube.com/watch?v=550X5OZVk7Y&t=99s.

Kerr, Dara. "Uber's Head Dealmaker Resigns after Reports of Sexual Misconduct." CNET, October 22, 2018.

https://www.cnet.com/news/ubers-head-dealmaker-resigns-after-reports-of-sexual-misconduct/.

Kharpal, Arjun. "5 Reasons Why Uber Sold Its China Business to Didi Chuxing." CNBC, August 1, 2016. https://www.cnbc.com/2016/08/01/5-reasons-why-uber-sold-its-china-business-to-didi-chuxing.html.

---. "Taxi App Rival Didi Chuxing to Buy Uber's China Business in $35 Billion Deal." CNBC, August 1, 2016. https://www.cnbc.com/2016/08/01/chinas-didi-chuxing-to-acquire-ubers-chinese-operations-wsj.html.

---. "Uber Settles for $100 Million in Lawsuit over Driver Status." CNBC, April 22, 2016. https://www.cnbc.com/2016/04/22/uber-makes-100-million-settlement-in-lawsuit-over-driver-status.html.

Kircher, Madison Malone. "How Uber Got Here." *New York Magazine*, March 8, 2017. http://nymag.com/intelligencer/article/dramatic-history-ride-hailing-app-uber-and-ceo-kalanick.html.

Kolodny, Lora. "Uber and Infosys Co-founders

Are Latest Billionaires to Join the Giving Pledge." CNBC, November 22, 2017. https://www.cnbc.com/2017/11/22/uber-and-infosys-co-founders-join-the-giving-pledge.html.

---. "UberCab, Now Just Uber, Shares Cease-and-Desist Orders." TechCrunch, accessed March 11, 2019. https://techcrunch.com/2010/10/25/ubercab-now-just-uber-shares-cease-and-desist-orders/.

---. "UberCab Ordered to Cease and Desist." TechCrunch, accessed March 11, 2019. https://techcrunch.com/2010/10/24/ubercab-ordered-to-cease-and-desist/.

Kosoff, Maya. "Everything You Need to Know about 'The Fountainhead,' a Book That Inspires Billionaire Uber CEO Travis Kalanick," Business Insider, June 1, 2015, https://www.businessinsider.com/how-ayn-rand-inspired-uber-ceo-travis-kalanick-2015-6?IR=T.

---. "A Look Inside the Insanely Successful Life of Billionaire Uber CEO Travis Kalanick." Business Insider, July 6, 2015. https://www.businessinsider.com/inside-the-successful-life-of-billionaire-uber-ceo-travis-kalanick-2015-7?IR=T.

---. "Travis Kalanick's First Company Got Sued for $250 Billion—So He Started a New 'Revenge Business' That Made Him a Millionaire." Business Insider, September 8, 2015. https://www.businessinsider.com/travis-kalanicks-first-company-got-sued-for-250-billion-so-he-started-a-new-revenge-business-that-made-him-a-millionaire-2015-9?IR=T.

---. "An Uber Campaign That Promised to Pair Customers with 'Hot Chick' Drivers in France Has Been Scrubbed." Business Insider, October 23, 2014. https://www.businessinsider.com/uber-avions-de-chasse-promotion-with-hot-chick-drivers-2014-10?IR=T.

Lacy, Sarah. "The Horrific Trickle Down of Asshole Culture: Why I've Just Deleted Uber from My Phone." Pando, October 22, 2014. https://pando.com/2014/10/22/the-horrific-trickle-down-of-asshole-culture-at-a-company-like-uber/.

---. "Venture Capital and the Great Big Silicon Valley Asshole Game." Pando, October 6, 2014. https://pando.com/2014/10/06/venture-capital-and-the-great-big-silicon-valley-asshole-game/.

Lashinsky, Adam. "Uber: An Oral History."
Fortune, June 3, 2015.
http://fortune.com/2015/06/03/uber-an-oral-history/.

Levenson, Eric. "Uber Driver Who Killed 6 in
Kalamazoo, Michigan, Shooting Rampage
Sentenced to Life in Prison." CNN, February 5,
2019.
https://edition.cnn.com/2019/02/05/us/uber
-driver-killer-kalamazoo/index.html.

Levin, Sam. "Uber's Scandals, Blunders, and
PR Disasters: The Full List," *Guardian*, June
28, 2017,
https://www.theguardian.com/technology/201
7/jun/18/uber-travis-kalanick-scandal-pr-
disaster-timeline.

Levine, Dan. "Uber Drivers Granted Class
Action Status in Lawsuit over Employment."
Reuters, September 1, 2015.
https://www.reuters.com/article/us-uber-
tech-drivers-lawsuit-
idUSKCN0R14O920150901.

LeWebParis. "5 Things to Know about LeWeb."
Accessed March 11, 2019.
https://www.lewebparis.com/things-to-know-

about-leweb/.

Liao, Shannon. "Uber Eats Rolls Out Confusing New Fees—Here's What They Mean." Verge, March 19, 2019. https://www.theverge.com/2019/3/19/182727 91/uber-eats-new-booking-delivery-service-fees-confusion-meaning.

Lomas, Natasha. "Uber Loses Its License to Operate." TechCrunch, September 22, 2017. https://techcrunch.com/2017/09/22/uber-loses-its-license-to-operate-in-london/.

Lopez, German. "Why People Are Deleting Uber from Their Phones after Trump's Executive Order." Vox, January 29, 2017. https://www.vox.com/policy-and-politics/2017/1/29/14431246/uber-trump-muslim-ban.

Lowensohn, Josh. "Uber Gutted Carnegie Mellon's Top Robotics Lab to Build Self-driving Cars." Verge, May 19, 2015. https://www.theverge.com/transportation/20 15/5/19/8622831/uber-self-driving-cars-carnegie-mellon-poached.

Lynch, Dennis. "Pizza Will Be Served: Inside Travis Kalanick's Real Estate Revolution." Real Deal, May 7, 2018.

https://therealdeal.com/la/2018/05/07/pizza-will-be-served-inside-travis-kalanicks-real-estate-revolution/.

Mango Research. "How Did Uber Start? The Birth of Travis Kalanick and Garrett Camp's Uber." April 8, 2017. YouTube video, 6:35. https://www.youtube.com/watch?v=wDgCNCd7KzY.

Marinova, Polina. "10 Things You Need to Know from Eric Holder's Uber Report." *Fortune*, June 13, 2017. http://fortune.com/2017/06/13/uber-internal-investigation-results-public/.

Marshall, Aarian. "1 Year after Uber's Fatal Crash, Robocars Carry On Quietly." Wired, March 18, 2019. https://www.wired.com/story/uber-crash-elaine-herzberg-anniversary-safety-self-driving/.

McGarry, Caitlin. "Burner Phones and Cancelled Rides: How Uber Steals Drivers from Lyft." PC World, August 27, 2014/. https://www.pcworld.com/article/2599506/burner-phones-and-canceled-rides-how-uber-steals-drivers-from-lyft.html.

Molla, Rani, and Theodore Schleifer. "Here's

Who Controls Uber after Its Megadeal with SoftBank." Recode, January 8, 2018. https://www.recode.net/2018/1/8/16865598/ uber-softbank-control-board-power-stocks-benchmark-travis-kalanick-dara-khosrowshahi.

Morales, Neil Jerome. "Philippine Watchdog Fine Grab, Uber for Rushed Merger, Drop in Service Quality." Reuters, October 17, 2018. https://www.reuters.com/article/us-uber-grab-philippines/philippine-watchdog-fines-grab-uber-for-rushed-merger-drop-in-service-quality-idUSKCN1MR146.

---. "Philippines Sets Rules for 'Virtual Monopolist' Grab after Uber Deal." Reuters, August 10, 2018. https://www.reuters.com/article/us-uber-grab-philippines/philippines-sets-rules-for-virtual-monopolist-grab-after-uber-deal-idUSKBN1KV0VI.

Moss, Caroline. "Uber CEO Defends His Company after a Driver Is Accused of Assaulting a Passenger." Business Insider, September 16, 2013. https://www.businessinsider.com/ubers-ceo-travis-kalanick-defends-driver-in-assault-2013-9?IR=T.

Newcomer, Eric. "Uber and Travis Kalanick Are in Business Again. This Time, as Competitors." Bloomberg, March 11, 2019. https://www.bloomberg.com/news/articles/2019-03-11/uber-and-travis-kalanick-are-in-business-again-this-time-as-competitors.

---. "Uber Paid Hackers to Delete Stolen Data on 57 Million People." Bloomberg, November 22, 2017. https://www.bloomberg.com/news/articles/2017-11-21/uber-concealed-cyberattack-that-exposed-57-million-people-s-data.

---, and Bloomberg. "Uber IPO Could Be One of Five Biggest NYSE Listings in History." *Fortune*, March 21, 2019. http://fortune.com/2019/03/21/uber-ipo-nyse-listing-lyft-nasdaq/.

---, and Joel Rosenblatt. "Here's the Uber Investor Letter That Forced Travis Kalanick Out." Bloomberg, January 28, 2019. https://www.bloomberg.com/news/articles/2019-01-28/here-s-the-uber-investor-letter-that-forced-travis-kalanick-out.

---, and Brad Stone. "The Fall of Travis Kalanick Was a Lot Weirder and Darker Than You Thought." *Bloomberg Businessweek*, January 18, 2018.

https://www.bloomberg.com/news/features/2 018-01-18/the-fall-of-travis-kalanick-was-a- lot-weirder-and-darker-than-you-thought.

Noack, Rick. "Anti-Uber Protests in France Lead to Scenes of Chaos and Violence." Washington Post, June 25, 2015. https://www.washingtonpost.com/news/worl dviews/wp/2015/06/25/anti-uber-protests-in- france-lead-to-scenes-of-chaos-and- violence/?utm_term=.b4f3dc4e415c.

O'Donnell, Carl, and Heather Somerville. "Exclusive: Uber Plans to Kick Off IPO in April—Sources." Reuters, March 14, 2019. https://www.reuters.com/article/us-uber-ipo- exclusive/exclusive-uber-plans-to-kick-off-ipo- in-april-sources-idUSKCN1QV2QU.

O'Kane, Sean. "Uber Is Testing an On-demand Staffing Business Called Uber Works." Verge, October 18, 2018. https://www.theverge.com/2018/10/18/17995 398/uber-works-staffing-business-test-trial.

Osborne, Charlie. "Uber, Lyft Return to Austin as Driver Fingerprint Rule Overturned." ZDNet, May 30, 2017. https://www.zdnet.com/article/uber-lyft- return-to-austin-as-texas-fingerprint-rule- dismissed/.

Peterson, Becky. "7 People You Never Realized Were Early Investors in Uber." Business Insider by Pulse, December 30, 2018. https://www.pulse.com.gh/bi/tech/7-people-you-never-realized-were-early-investors-in-uber/9n6z1c8.

Primack, Dan. "Scoop: Benchmark Capital Sues Travis Kalanick for Fraud." Axios, August 10, 2017. https://www.axios.com/scoop-benchmark-capital-sues-travis-kalanick-for-fraud-1513304764-18c62fe5-c80e-4fec-ad1b-135ffaafa1ec.html.

Quinn, Ben. "Uber UK Strike: Users Urged Not to Cross 'Digital Picket Line.'" *Guardian*, October 9, 2018. https://www.theguardian.com/technology/2018/oct/09/uber-uk-strike-users-urged-not-to-cross-digital-picket-line.

Rai, Saritha. "Uber Gets Serious about Passenger Safety in India, Introduces Panic Button." *Forbes*, February 12, 2015. https://www.forbes.com/sites/saritharai/2015/02/12/uber-gets-serious-about-passenger-safety-in-india-introduces-panic-button/#174118aa3cf8.

Randazzo, Ryan. "Family of Woman Killed in Crash with Self-Driving Uber Sues Arizona,

Tempe." *AZ Central*, March 19, 2019. https://www.azcentral.com/story/news/local/tempe/2019/03/19/arizona-city-tempe-sued-family-uber-self-driving-car-crash-victim-elaine-herzberg/3207598002/.

Rapkin, Mickey. "Uber Cab Confessions." *GQ*, February 27, 2014. https://www.gq.com/story/uber-cab-confessions.

Raymond, Chris. "Travis Kalanick: 'You Can Either Do What They Say or You Can Fight for What You Believe." Success, February 13, 2017. https://www.success.com/travis-kalanick-you-can-either-do-what-they-say-or-you-can-fight-for-what-you-believe/.

Reilly, Katie. "Every Event That Led to Uber CEO Travis Kalanick's Resignation." *Fortune*, June 21, 2017. http://fortune.com/2017/06/21/uber-controversy-timeline-travis-kalanick/.

Regan, James, and John Irish. "France Cracks Down on Uber after Taxi Driver Protests." Reuters, June 25, 2015. https://www.reuters.com/article/us-france-uber-idUSKBN0P50RX20150625.

Reuters. "Uber CEO Travis Kalanick Will Take

Indefinite Leave of Absence." June 13, 2017. http://fortune.com/2017/06/13/uber-ceo-travis-kalanick-leave-of-absence/.

---. "Uber Settles with Family of Woman Killed by Self-Driving Car." *Guardian*, March 29, 2019. https://www.theguardian.com/technology/2018/mar/29/uber-settles-with-family-of-woman-killed-by-self-driving-car.

Rosenbaum, Eric. "Get Ready for the $200 Billion IPO Shakeup in 2019." CNBC, December 17, 2018. https://www.cnbc.com/2018/12/14/get-ready-for-the-200-billion-ipo-shakeup-in-2019.html.

Russell, Jon. "Indonesia's Kargo Comes Out of Stealth with $7.6 Million from Travis Kalanick, Sequoia, and Others." TechCrunch, March 22, 2019. https://techcrunch.com/2019/03/22/kargo/.

Sanikop, Leela. "9 Investments That Will Help Make Jay-Z the First Billionaire in Hip-hop." Moguldom, June 2, 2017. https://moguldom.com/7240/9-investments-that-will-help-make-jay-z-the-first-billionaire-in-hip-hop/2/.

Sarkar, Pooja, and Ashna Ambre. "Uber Raises

up to $100 Million from Tata Fund." Live Mint, August 20, 2015. https://www.livemint.com/Companies/3stUS qNMHesUdVi8NmLXTK/Uber-gets-investment-from-Tata-Capital-Fund-to-expand-in-Ind.html.

Schonfeld, Erick. "Uber CEO on His 'Official' NYC Launch: 'Congestion Is a Bitch' (Video and Heatmaps)." TechCrunch, accessed March 11, 2019. https://techcrunch.com/2011/05/04/uber-screenshots-video/.

Schulze, Elizabeth. "Uber Fined Nearly $1.2 Million by British and Dutch Authorities for 2016 Data Breach." CNBC, November 27, 2018. https://www.cnbc.com/2018/11/27/uber-fined-more-than-1-million-dollars-by-uk-and-dutch-authorities.html.

SEO. "Oscar Salazar." Accessed March 16, 2019. https://www.seo-usa.org/about/board-of-directors/oscar-salazar/.

Shankland, Stephen. "Car Service Uber Raises $32 Million, Launches in Paris." CNET, December 7, 2011. https://www.cnet.com/news/car-service-uber-raises-32-million-launches-in-paris/.

Shieber, Jonathan. "Travis Kalanick Is Launching a Venture Fund." TechCrunch, March 7, 2018, https://techcrunch.com/2018/03/07/travis-kalanick-is-launching-a-venture-fund/.

Shontell, Alyson. "All Hail the Uber Man! How Sharp-Elbowed Salesman Travis Kalanick Became Silicon Valley's Newest Star." Business Insider, January 11, 2014. https://www.businessinsider.com/uber-travis-kalanick-bio-2014-1?IR=T.

Smith, Ben. "Uber Executive Suggests Digging Up Dirt on Journalists." BuzzFeed, November 17, 2014. https://www.buzzfeednews.com/article/bensmith/uber-executive-suggests-digging-up-dirt-on-journalists#.yoNAxXY1m.

Smith, Tim J. "Uber Is Finally Growing Up." *Fortune*, August 22, 2017. http://fortune.com/2018/08/22/uber-ceo-new-york-london/.

Somerville, Heather. "SoftBank Is Now Uber's Largest Shareholder as Deal Closes." Reuters, January 18, 2018. https://www.reuters.com/article/us-uber-softbank-tender/softbank-is-now-ubers-largest-shareholder-as-deal-closesidUSKBN1F72WL.

---. "Uber Director David Bonderman Resigns from Board Following Comment about Women." Reuters, June 14, 2017. https://www.reuters.com/article/us-uber-bonderman-idUSKBN195053.

Stone, Brad. "Uber: The App That Changed How the World Hails a Taxi." *Guardian*, January 29, 2017. https://www.theguardian.com/technology/2017/jan/29/uber-app-changed-how-world-hails-a-taxi-brad-stone/.

Swisher, Kara. "StumbleUpon Stumbles Out of eBay's Arms to Be Reborn as a Startup (Plus the Entire Press Release)." All Things Digital, April 13, 2009. http://allthingsd.com/20090413/stumbleupon-stumbles-out-of-ebays-arms-to-be-reborn-as-a-start-up/.

---, and Johana Bhuiyan. "Uber CEO Kalanick Advised Employees on Sex Rules for a Company Celebration in 2013 'Miami Letter.'" Recode, June 8, 2017. https://www.recode.net/2017/6/8/15765514/2013-miami-letter-uber-ceo-kalanick-employees-sex-rules-company-celebration.

---. "Uber's VP of Product and Growth Ed Baker Has Resigned." Recode, March 3, 2017. https://www.recode.net/2017/3/3/14805384/uber-ed-baker-resigns-travis-kalanick.

Tata Opportunities Fund. "About." Accessed March 11, 2019. https://www.tataopportunitiesfund.com/about-us.html.

Taylor, Kate. "40 of the Biggest Scandals in Uber History." Business Insider, November 24, 2017. https://www.businessinsider.com/uber-company-scandals-and-controversies-2017-11?IR=T.

TechCrunch. "eBay's StumbleUpon Acquisition: Confirmed at $75 Million." Accessed March 11, 2019. https://techcrunch.com/2007/05/30/ebays-stumbleupon-acquisition-confirmed-at-75-million/.

Tepper, Fitz. "Uber Cofounder Garret Camp Is Creating a New Cryptocurrency." TechCrunch, March 1, 2018. https://techcrunch.com/2018/03/01/uber-co-founder-garrett-camp-is-creating-a-new-cryptocurrency/.

Than, Krisztina, and Krisztina Fenyo. "Uber to

Suspend Operations in Hungary Due to
Government Legislation." Reuters, July 13,
2016. https://www.reuters.com/article/us-
uber-hungary-exit/uber-to-suspend-
operations-in-hungary-due-to-govt-legislation-
idUSKCN0ZT0RS.

Tiku, Nitasha. "Uber CEO on Driver 'Assault':
It's Not Real and We're Not Responsible."
Valleywag, September 16, 2013.
http://valleywag.gawker.com/uber-ceo-on-
driver-assault-its-not-real-and-were-n-
1323533057.

Trefis Team. "How Uber Could Justify a $120
Billion Valuation." *Forbes*, December 3, 2018.
https://www.forbes.com/sites/greatspeculatio
ns/2018/12/03/how-uber-could-justify-a-120-
billion-valuation/#d8ef0fa7f9b3.

Uber. "Dara Khosrowshahi." Accessed March
11, 2019. https://www.uber.com/en-
KE/newsroom/leadership/dara-
khosrowshahi/.

---. "Facts & Figures." Accessed March 11,
2019. https://www.uber.com/en-
KE/newsroom/company-info/.

---. "The Future of Transportation." Accessed
March 11, 2019.

https://www.uber.com/info/atg/.

---. "History." Accessed March 11, 2019, https://www.uber.com/en-KE/newsroom/history/.

Venzon, Cliff. "Uber to End Service in the Philippines on Monday." *Nikkei Asian Review*, April 16, 2018. https://asia.nikkei.com/Business/Companies/Uber-Grab-moves-closer-to-Southeast-Asian-integration.

Villas-Boas, Antonio. "StumbleUpon, the Addictive Internet Tool Made by an Uber Cofounder Who Brought You to Random Sites, Is Folding." Business Insider, May 24, 2018. https://www.businessinsider.com/stumbleupon-is-shutting-down-2018-5?IR=T.

What Success. "Garrett Camp." Accessed March 11, 2019. http://whatsuccess.com/success-story-garrett-camp/.

Wolff, Michael. "Wolff: Behind the Scenes at Uber/BuzzFeed Fracas." *USA Today*, November 19, 2014. https://www.usatoday.com/story/money/columnist/wolff/2014/11/19/behind-the-scenes-uber-buzzfeed-fracas/19269737/.

Wong, Julia Carrie. "Ex-Uber CEO Travis Kalanick Reveals New Project: a 'Job Creation' Fund." *Guardian*, March 8, 2018. https://www.theguardian.com/business/2018/mar/07/uber-ceo-travis-kalanick-10100-investment-fund.

---. "Uber CEO Steps Down from Trump Advisory Council after Users Boycott." *Guardian*, February 3, 2017. https://www.theguardian.com/technology/2017/feb/02/travis-kalanick-delete-uber-leaves-trump-council.

---. "Uber CEO Travis Kalanick Caught on Video Arguing with Driver about Fares." Guardian, March 1, 2017. "https://www.theguardian.com/technology/2017/feb/28/uber-ceo-travis-kalanick-driver-argument-video-fare-prices.

Zanona, Melanie, and David McCabe. "Uber's Drive to Be a DC Powerhouse." *Hill*, January 25, 2017. https://thehill.com/policy/transportation/315960-ubers-drive-to-be-a-dc-powerhouse.

Zart, Nicolas. "Uber Elevate: Future of Air Taxis = 3 Hours of Flight, 150 MPH, 4 Passengers." Clean Technica, February 15, 2019.

https://cleantechnica.com/2019/02/15/uber-elevate-future-of-air-taxis-3-hours-of-flight-150-mph-4-passengers/.

Made in the USA
Las Vegas, NV
01 October 2022